MW01054615

₵ℙℬ The Practitioner's Bookshelf

Hands-On Literacy Books for
Classroom Teachers and Administrators

Dorothy S. Strickland
FOUNDING EDITOR, LANGUAGE AND LITERACY SERIES

Celia Genishi and Donna E. Alvermann
LANGUAGE AND LITERACY SERIES EDITORS*

* For a list of current titles in the Language and Literacy Series, see *www.tcpress.com*

Let's Poem

The Essential Guide to Teaching Poetry in a High-Stakes, Multimodal World

MARK DRESSMAN

Foreword by Nikki Giovanni

Teachers College, Columbia University
New York and London

Permission Acknowledgments:

Excerpt from "Elena" from "Chants" by Pat Mora is reprinted with permission from the publisher (© 1994 Arte Público Press–University of Houston).

Excerpt from "Dracula" by Salwa Al-Neimi is used by permission of the translator, Shawkat Toorawa.

"Identity Crisis" from *The Return of the Blue Cat*, by F. D. Reeve. New York: Other Press, 2005, pp. 4–6, © F. D. Reeve, 2005.

Excerpt from "What the Angels Left," is used by permission of author Marie Howe.

"Poem (For Nina)" © 1972 by Nikki Giovanni from *My House* by permission of the author.

Excerpt from "Po' Boy Blues" from *The Collected Works of Langston Hughes* by Langston Hughes, edited by Arnold Rampersad with David Roessel, Associate Editor, copyright © 1994 by the Estate of Langston Hughes. Used by permission of Alfred A. Knopf, a Division of Random House, Inc.

Excerpt from "We Real Cool" by Gwendolyn Brooks is reprinted by consent of Brooks Permissions.

Published by Teachers College Press, 1234 Amsterdam Avenue, New York, NY 10027

Copyright © 2010 by Teachers College, Columbia University

All rights reserved. No part of this publication may be reproduced or transmitted in any form or by any means, electronic or mechanical, including photocopy, or any information storage and retrieval system, without permission from the publisher.

Library of Congress Cataloging-in-Publication Data

Dressman, Mark.
    Let's poem : the essential guide to teaching poetry in a high-stakes, multimodal world / Mark Dressman.
        p. cm. — (The practitioner's bookshelf series)
    Includes bibliographical references and index.
    ISBN 978-0-8077-5139-8 (pbk. : alk. paper)
        1. Poetry—Study and teaching (Secondary)—United States. 2. Poetry—Authorship—Study and teaching (Secondary)—United States. 3. Poetry and the Internet—United States. I. Title.
    PN1101.D77   2010
    808.1071'2—dc22   2010017654

ISBN 978-0-8077-5139-8 (paper)

Printed on acid-free paper
Manufactured in the United States of America

17   16   15   14   13   12   11   10   8   7   6   5   4   3   2   1

For Mac

Who's a poet,

But doesn't know it.

Contents

Foreword

Who would have thought
There would be/could be a button
On the wall
Where when you touch
The room lights up
Electricity didn't build
On the candle
It replaced wax

Who would want to believe
Human beings could sit
On a Hydrogen Bomb
(we call it a Space Ship)
    and sail off into Space
    and walk on the moon
    and land a surrogate on Mars
Just to Marvel! at the unknown
And why wouldn't
We want to take what is
    Known
And add what is
    Wonderful
And let the poems flow
    From tears of laughter
    From sweat of work
    From the deliciousness of tomorrow
To the knowledge of Today

Grant me that A implies B
B necessitates C
C calls for D

And eventually
And you and I will get an Alphabet

Grant me that Curiosity implies Research
Research requires Reading
Reading delights the heart
And you and I will get a voice

Grant me Love implies
     not desire but Commitment
Commitment accepts Challenge

Challenge embraces Theory
And you and I will get Reason: A way to
                                        explore past
                                        actions
                                            and
                                        future dreams

Good for us
On your Mark Dressman Get Ready!
Let's Poem!

—Nikki Giovanni,
Poet and University Distinguished Professor, Virginia Tech

Acknowledgments

This book is the product of 3 decades of teaching and learning from students and colleagues in many schools and universities, but especially from five teachers and the students in five schools in Central Illinois representing a wide range of cultures, settings, and grades. To Ms. Hendrick, Ms. Parker, Ms. Lewis, Mr. Riordan, Ms. Clinton (all pseudonyms), and the students whose work is quoted in this book and the many more whose work was not able to be published, I am extremely grateful for your generosity of time and interest and your patience in scheduling class sessions and waiting for the book to be published. Many students in the secondary English education program at the University of Illinois at Urbana-Champaign also contributed their time, energy, and enthusiasm to teaching the approaches described in this book: Jeff Wagner, Emily Ritter, Rachel Hahn, Caleb Curtiss, Jennifer Roemer, Brittany Balazs, Deanna Barthel, Laura Koritz, Jackie Wiedemann, Elizabeth Plog, Sarah Hively, and Caitlin Megginson. Without their help in coordinating and teaching, many insights and examples would have been lost. Finally, I am grateful for a Hardie Collaborative Research Stipend from the College of Education at UIUC that made much of the teaching in the five classrooms possible.

I am also extremely grateful to the professional poets, and particularly to the contemporary poets whose generosity and interest in the book made the publication of lines and in two cases entire poems possible. Pat Mora, Marie Howe, and Shawkat Toorawa, translator of Salwa Al-Neimi's poem, "Dracula," were all very responsive and quick to offer their permission for reprint of portions of their poems. Franklin Reeve was especially generous in offering suggestions and the entire text of his poem, "Identity Crisis," for publication in Chapter 1. Finally, I am very grateful for the example and the art and now humbled by the support of Nikki Giovanni, whose "Poem (For Nina)" has been the inspiration for many "skin poems" over my teaching career. Thank you also to her associate, Virginia Fowler at Virginia Tech, for her support in coordinating our correspondence.

Last, I thank my son, Mac, for the fun we had on the car ride back to the hotel in California last summer when we "went random" and tried to surprise each other with our irrelevance, and to my wife Sarah for another summer of writing.

Introduction

POETRY RORSCHACH

Here are the opening lines of three poems:

> When to the sessions of sweet silent thought
> I summon up remembrance of things past,
> I sigh the lack of many a thing I sought,
> And with old woes new wail my dear time's waste . . .
> —William Shakespeare, from *Sonnet 30*

> "Will you walk a little faster?" said a whiting to a snail.
> "There's a porpoise close behind us, and he's treading on
> my tail.

See how eagerly the lobsters and the turtles all advance!
They are waiting on the shingle—will you come and join
        the dance?"
        —Lewis Carroll, from *Alice's Adventures in Wonderland*

My Spanish isn't enough.
I remember how I'd smile
listening to my little ones,
understanding every word they'd say,
their jokes, their songs, their plots . . .
                                    —Pat Mora, from *Elena*

How would you teach these poems to a class of early to mid-adolescents? Would you assume their presentation as a group signals some hidden structural and thematic connection—so your task as a teacher would be to identify those connections and then craft questions to lead students to discover them? Or would you take a more open-ended approach, letting students choose whether to read the poems individually or as a set?

Perhaps you decide these poems have no relation to one another and should be taught individually. Would you follow the same approach for each poem, or vary your instruction? You might focus on the form of the Shakespearean sonnet, noting the regularity of the rhyme, meter, and stanzas for the first poem and in conclusion ask individual students or the whole class to write a sonnet of their own. You might build on the humor and lightness of the Lewis Carroll piece and invite students to practice reading it aloud or act the poem out. And finally, you might note the emotion of the Mora poem, inviting students perhaps to reflect in writing on how they would feel in this situation or if they knew someone whose mother did not speak English.

I call this exercise a "Poetry Rorschach." Like the inkblots on paper that psychologists use diagnostically, there are no right or wrong answers to these questions. Our responses reveal underlying dispositions, attitudes, and concerns. But whereas inkblots are intended to reveal what is unique within one's psyche, how someone interprets the task of teaching three very different poems probably has more to say about historical and cultural dilemmas in literacy and literature education.

Hermann Rorschach (1884–1922) was the son of a Swiss art teacher who was fascinated in high school by *Klecksography*, a form of art consisting of symmetrical inkblot images. As a medical student at the University of Zurich he studied with noted psychoanalysts and developed his psychological test, based on the premise that people's responses to inkblots revealed much about their inner psychological state. The term "Rorschach" today is a metaphor for any event or activity that appears to reveal the underlying motives or logic of a group.

Since at least early in the last century, classroom teachers, curriculum specialists, and researchers have struggled and typically failed to resolve the issue of how best to bring adolescents and poetry together. In a study of 530 articles on the teaching of poetry that were published in *English Journal* between 1912 and 2005, my colleague at the University of Georgia, Mark Faust, and I found that from the earliest days of the journal until the early 1970s, a debate raged between two opposing points of view about poetry. On one side, many university professors and some teachers urged a *formalist*, or as it was known from the 1930s through the 1960s, a New Critical approach, in which poems were treated as "jewels" of language to be studied in great detail, outside of their social context and for their own sake.

New Criticism is the school of literary theory that predominated in university—and, by extension, secondary school—English departments from the 1920s through the 1960s. New Critics focus on "close readings" of texts—in which grammar, style, and word choice form the basis for determining the possible thematic meanings of a text—and focus closely on textual details, rather than on the text as a general whole. The theory was criticized and lost influence beginning in the late 1960s because it deliberately excludes examining the biographical, social, and historical context in which a text was written or is read, as well as readers' "affective" (emotional) responses to the text. Yet many New Critical practices, such as a close focus on the linguistic elements of literary texts and the identification of symbolism and theme, remain mainstays of literary analysis and education to this day.

On the other side, many teachers and the occasional university professor advocated a *populist* approach, in which poems were regarded as the possession of the reader, and were fair game for a wide range of activities, including writing parodies of them, dramatizing them, illustrating them, and using them as touchstones for reflective and creative writing activities. Both sides also attacked each other's position, with formalists accusing populists of trivializing poetry and language study, and populists noting at every opportunity how much students hated poetry when it was taught formally.

Since the 1970s attention to poetry has waned within the field of English education and has continued to lag ever since. Publications advocating Formalist approaches in secondary education have disappeared almost entirely. Fewer Populist articles have also been published, although in many cases those published have offered innovative new ideas. Publications in the new millennium have focused on writing and sometimes performing new forms, such as spoken word, hip-hop, and rap, and multimodal/digital poetry.

The Formalist Position:

"That every student early in his high-school course should learn the simpler matters of metrics, together with illustrative lines, and should learn them as thoroughly as ever he did his multiplication tables, seems to me so obvious as scarcely to need statement."

—Harry G. Paul,
"The Teaching of Lyric Poetry," 1912

The Populist Position:

"The need for teaching literary appreciation in the schools is beginning to be generally recognized, although university-bred instructors to some extent still insist on foisting upon their unhappy high-school charges the methods of university scholarship. . . . It is my experience that in the effort to catch the spirit and lilt of Omar (Khayyam) by trying to write in his style, (the student) invariably gains more in the way of actually understanding than do those who merely write an essay about Omar."

—Frank W. Chandler,
"A Creative Approach to the Study of Literature," 1915

The Lasting Debate:
Then as Now?

"I don't believe in teaching poetry. I don't even know what it is—or, if I do, how to communicate it. . . . On the other hand, I believe strongly in teaching poems—many of them. And, I believe, too often the teaching of poems suffers because of a teacher's vain attempt to teach 'poetry.' Furthermore, the chief obstacle to teaching poems is often the actual vehicle of teaching 'poetry.' I refer to the so-called 'poetry unit.'"

—Margaret B. Ackerman,
"Why I Don't Teach Poetry," 1968

"Many of our current dilemmas are probably due to the increased permissiveness of a society which puts few demands (mental or physical) on its children, a society in which the term *discipline* can only be used by faculty members susurrating timidly behind closed doors."

—Don Gutteridge,
"The Affective Fallacy and the Student's Response to Poetry," 1972

"In contrast, we believe that 'students-as-producers-of-technologies' engage in much more meaningful learning than students-as-receivers-from-instructional-technologies (Jonassen, Peck, & Wilson, 1999). Consequently, we decided to teach our poetry units using media and hypermedia."

—Peter Dreher,
"Electronic Poetry: Student-Constructed Hypermedia," 2000

"While poets may shake off metrical regularities that they might well find shackling, they still aim to make the most of their medium—to fit sound to idea, to find coherence in language that matches coherence in thought. Listening with open ears, students can hear, understand, and enjoy the jazz rhythms of a Langston Hughes or the syncopations of e.e. cummings or the subjective instabilities of such diverse voices as Walt Whitman, Anne Sexton, Robert Lowell, and Adrienne Rich."

—Lewis Cobbs, "Learning to Listen, Listening to Learn:
Teaching Poetry as a Sensory Medium," 2005

However, aside from publications focusing on spoken word poetry and multimodality, the comparative lack of serious attention to poetry in the English curriculum in this century, compared to its heyday in the first half of the 20th, is striking. What happened? Has the debate been resolved with Populism the victor, or was it merely tabled? The responses I receive from preservice teachers to the Poetry Rorschach activity suggest that English educators are still locked in the grip of the debate. In other words, it seems that when teaching the poetry of the past, one still must decide whether to pay tedious attention to every accent, word ending, and phrase in a poem, with the result that students learn to hate poetry, or to focus on personal response and "fun" activities with poems, with the result that students may learn to ignore or dismiss much of the complexity and nuance within poetic texts.

POETRY'S IMPORTANCE FOR LITERACY EDUCATION

The failure to resolve this dilemma is very unfortunate, for two reasons. First, without a continuing conversation about how best to teach it, poetry receives little attention in most English classrooms today. Poems are typically taught in isolation, as fillers between novels and plays, or as short units meant to "cover" the genre as quickly as possible. Yet most of the world's literature prior to the 19th century in Great Britain and the United States, and even still today in much of the world, is poetic in its form and language.

Second, despite all their problems, the New Critics did get one thing right. They argued that for teaching and learning how to make inferences, find the main idea, support a claim with details, distinguish between the literal and the figurative, and generally to read carefully, or *closely* as they put it, no other form of text beats the lyric poem for portability, craftedness, or the capacity to engage, entertain, and even awe. How ironic, then, in an era when teachers are being pressed as never before to teach directly to the reading skills measured by standardized tests, that the form of literature best suited in many ways to teaching and learning these skills is the one that is often least emphasized and least taught in English language arts classrooms.

PURPOSE OF THE BOOK

This book is dedicated to two propositions.

First, teachers shouldn't and don't have to be tied to histori-cal impulses either to teach poetry as bad-tasting medicine that is "good for you," or as "word candy" that dissolves pleasantly in the mouth without leaving much of a "nutritional," or academic, trace. Instead, the practices described in the next chapters draw from the best of both traditions. They work to engage students in writing, re-writing multimodally (or "remixing"), and performing poems from their own and from classical poetic traditions in ways that require them, within the process and so within a meaningful context, to learn the forms—the meters, the rhyme schemes, the stanza forms, and the types of figurative expressions and their purposes—that make careful reading of all sorts of crafted texts both pleasurable and profitable.

This principle moves poetry beyond the status of a "genre" to be taught as a self-contained unit, to something to be integrated within the context of an entire year or more of study. With this concept, the focus of activity is engagement with poetic language and expres-sion , rather than poems or a particular poet—and that engagement often takes place in conjunction with the reading of more extended texts such as short stories and adolescent novels and plays, or as part of a broad range of texts read and written in conjunction with a theme that may be interdisciplinary.

Second, this book argues that the development of proficiency in the use of poetic forms of language and expression is not a luxury, but is an integral aspect of the increasingly wide range of literate skills and practices that students will be using in the 21st century. The time and energy spent in classrooms engaging in poetic forms of literacy are easily justifiable in terms of the standards, goals, and objectives for reading and the language arts that most if not all states and districts in the United States and provinces in Cana-da currently enforce through standardized, typically high-stakes, testing. Moreover, these skills and practices, particularly the ones developed through the activities of Chapters 5 and 6, align fully with the definition of 21st-Century Literacy recently proposed by the National Council of Teachers of English (www.ncte.org; search for "positions").

21st-Century Literacy

- Develops proficiency with the tools of technology
- Builds relationships with others to pose and solve problems collaboratively and cross-culturally
- Designs and shares information for global communities to meet a variety of purposes
- Manages, analyzes, and synthesizes multiple streams of simultaneous information
- Creates, critiques, analyzes, and evaluates multimedia texts
- Attends to the ethical responsibilities required by these complex environments.

Nationally, the teaching of poetry as a core reading and writing strategy is equally justifiable through state standards. In New York, Standard Two in grades 7 and 8 states that when writing, students will "select a genre and use appropriate conventions such as dialogue, rhythm, and rhyme"; when reading, students will "recognize how the author's use of language creates images or feelings," and "identify poetic elements such as repetition, rhythm, and rhyming patterns in order to interpret poetry." In California, Standard 1.1 of the grade 7 Core Standards calls for students to "identify idioms, analogies, metaphors, and similes in prose and poetry," and at grades 9 and 10 to "distinguish between denotative and connotative meanings of words and interpret the connotative power of words" (Standard 1.2), as well as "identify and assess the impact of perceived ambiguities, nuances, and complexities within the text" (Standard 2.4.a). Finally, in Texas, the Texas Essential Knowledge and Skills (TEKS) for grade 6 beginning in 2009 states that "students are expected to adjust fluency when reading aloud grade-level text based on the reading purpose and the nature of the text" (110.18.b.1), and that students will "use comprehension skills to analyze how words, images, graphics, and sounds work together in various forms to impact meaning" (110.18.b.13).

PLAN OF THE BOOK

The following chapters take up the challenge to realize the opportunities for expression and careful attention to language that poetry provides by "poaching" the most creative and academically sound principles and practices of both the formalist and populist traditions and "remixing" them in activities that are performative, expressive, and culturally relevant. These exercises also require students to engage in the intense study of the forms and functions of a range of poetic traditions, from the canonical work of Shakespeare, Keats, and Frost to the poets of the Harlem Renaissance, the Beats, and Hip-Hop, to the contemporary traditions of the Caribbean, Latin America, Africa, Asia, Australia, the Middle East, and Europe.

The approaches in the book have been "field-tested" in real classrooms. Throughout each chapter, the approaches are supported with references to online resources featuring poems, videos, and information about poets and the teaching of poetry. The simple links, or URLs, for these sites are provided directly in the text of the chapters, but an easier way to access the sites may be to go online to the website that supports this book: letspoemresources.ning.com. This website is designed not only as an easy way to access the dozens of websites referenced in this book, but also as a portal and social networking site for teaching poetry through performative, multimodal approaches. You'll be asked to sign up as a member; and once you've joined, you'll have access to all the links in the book plus a community of educators interested in the potential of poetry as an aesthetic *and* developmental experience for students.

Chapters 1 through 5 each feature a different approach to teaching poetry, along with resources for teachers interested in using the approach in their classrooms. These chapters are organized from approaches focusing on the most basic structural aspects of poetry to the most technical, in terms of knowledge of poetry (from intuition to declarative knowledge) and practices of expression (from oral interpretation to advanced uses of ubiquitously available software). As a whole, the five approaches can work as a "basic course" in poetry education. Chapter 1, "Choral Reading: Studying Rhythm, Inflection, and Meaning," synthesizes practices from a very old tradition in poetry education, "oral interpretation," and from the work of children's poet Paul Fleischman (e.g., *Joyful Noise:*

Poems for Two Voices, Fleischman & Beddows, 2004). However, rather than students memorizing and reciting a poem in class or reading a poem jointly that has already been "orchestrated" for them, in choral reading small groups of 2 to 4 students select a poem and orchestrate it themselves. When students are asked to explain their decisions, or when two groups differently orchestrate the same poem and the class discusses how differences in the orchestration affected the meaning of the poem, a powerful set of conditions for interpreting and analyzing a poem at very close range is created.

In Chapter 2, "Skin Poetry: Figuring Out Figurative Language," students use metaphors and similes to describe an object close to their experience. In two teachers' classrooms, students brainstormed descriptors for their skin—its color, its texture, and its symbolic meanings for them—and then used the figures of speech they created to write poems about their own skin and its meaning in their lives. After sharing their initial drafts, students read "Poem (For Nina)" by Nikki Giovanni, to study Giovanni's use of metaphor and spacing before revising their work on computers. Ways and resources for extending this approach to other topics, such as "math," "homework," or "hands," are also discussed, offering ways to teach poetry across the curriculum [and content areas?].

Chapter 3, "Blues Poetry and Other Forms of Cultural Expression," is grounded in a favorite activity that I have used as a middle-school teacher and as a teacher educator. Students in three classrooms identified the stanza form and rhyme scheme of blues poems and discussed the general plaintive and ironic tone of the poems, and then composed and performed a poem for the class on a topic such as "The Third Period English Blues," or "The Cafeteria Blues." They performed their poems as blues singers, complete with vocalized guitar riffs and clapping from the class. In the 20 years since I first developed this approach, it has never failed to elicit wild enthusiasm from both middle-school and English-education students. Additional forms, such as the *corrido* from the U.S.-Mexican borderlands or many different Asian forms, may also be taught through this approach.

Chapter 4, "Hip-Hop and Spoken Word: The Elements of Poetry," is written with three goals in mind. The first is to examine the poetic value of hip-hop forms of poetry, and to counter the stereotypical image of rap and hip-hop as inherently misogynistic and violent. The second is to demonstrate the power of hip-hop as an introduction to many of the structural elements of English poetry, including allusion, alliteration, rhyme, and meter (beat). The third goal is to provide a range of resources and pedagogical strategies for bringing hip-hop and spoken word into their classrooms. Students alternately write and perform their own poems, research particular hip-hop and spoken-word artists, or select and perform published hip-hop poems.

Chapter 5, "Digital Performance: Remixing the Masters Multi-modally," focuses on discussion of electronic formats that, as in Chapter 4, create powerful conditions for interpretation. In one approach, students in one classroom selected a favorite "classic" poem, such as "We Real Cool" by Gwendolyn Brooks, or a passage from *The Iliad*, while students in another classroom chose to animate their "skin poems" from the activity in Chapter 2 of this book. Using music, still and video recordings, and the advanced animation features of a ubiquitous program like PowerPoint (or iMovie or MovieMaker), students create a visual, iconic interpretation of the poem. The chapter provides relatively detailed steps for creating multimodally using both PCs and Macs and includes links to multiple online resources, including tutorials for several different software programs.

The concluding 6th chapter, "Global Voices Online: Internationalizing and Diversifying Your Curriculum," offers a wide range of online resources for teachers who may otherwise lack access to a range of poems or a knowledge of poetry and poetic traditions within and outside the United States, Great Britain, and Ireland. There are many excellent online sites devoted to conventional forms of poetry, to hip-hop, to individual poets, and to the poets and poetry of India, China, Latin America, and virtually every other region of the world. These resources are provided to encourage the introduction of multiple poetic traditions into the English curriculum, particularly in classrooms with immigrant student populations.

CHOOSE YOUR OWN COURSE: HOW TO USE THIS BOOK

In summary, this book is premised on two ideas: that teaching poetry performatively engages students' interests and develops analytical skill and knowledge in the basic structures of poetic language and expression simultaneously; and that in the course of this engagement, many of the skills and practices of reading, writing, and speaking typically listed in most U.S. state standards are also addressed. In other words, in teaching poetry through processes that require students to produce and perform interpretive readings and poems of their own, you need not put aside or ignore demands to "teach for the test."

Chapters 1 through 5 are devoted to approaches that meet this goal, while Chapter 6 provides a list of resources for teaching poetry as a global medium of communication and for reaching out to the increasing numbers of students in U.S. classrooms from international backgrounds. The first five chapters are organized from approaches focusing on the most basic structural aspects of poetry to the most technical, in terms of knowledge of poetry (from intuition to declarative knowledge) and practices of expression (from oral interpretation to advanced uses of commonly available software). As a whole, the five approaches may be seen to constitute a "basic course" in poetry education. However, each chapter stands independently from the others and the ideas in them may be used out of sequence. The invitation to you as a teacher of literacy, then, is to try out the approaches in sequential order or to skip around as individual circumstances might require. But no matter how you may choose to use the ideas in this book, in their use I urge you to take a fresh look at the power that having your students perform and produce readings of their own and others' poetry can have for their development as literate citizens of the 21st century.

Choral Reading

Studying Rhythm, Inflection, and Meaning

O ne of the oldest and perhaps most tried-and-true approaches for getting students to engage closely and repeatedly with the individual lines, phrases, and words of a poem is having them memorize and recite or simply rehearse the reading of a poem again and again. As early as 1913, Horace Eaton of Syracuse University, writing in *The English Journal* (later, *English Journal*), urged that students and teachers should practice reading poetry aloud to themselves and to their classes. In 1936, Ben Renz, a teacher at Ishpeming High School in Michigan, suggested a four-step process whereby students might be taught how to read and/or recite "effectively enough to become converted to poetry" (p. 563).

Choral reading was a far livelier practice in the United States in the 1930s and 1940s than it is today. It currently survives mainly in elementary schools as a means of improving reading fluency although at the secondary level many of its central practices, such as the scoring of verse and use of syncopated voices, are also central to group performances of spoken word and slam poetry. To judge from YouTube, choral reading/speaking thrives in its original format in many South Asian and East Asian nations today—particularly in Malaysia—as a competitive school activity.

In the United States, however, the practice of students giving practiced readings/recitations of poems aloud in front of a class or in an auditorium is likely to raise more eyebrows among teachers than strike an interest in them, for it conjures the image of a series of nervous, embarrassed students who haven't quite yet memorized or prepared the reading muddling through with the opposite of the intended effect. Indeed, of all the approaches teachers were offered to try during the research for this book, choral reading was the least often chosen.

Choral Reading and Speaking Online

A quick check of the Internet shows that choral reading and speaking currently has a strong presence in two main areas: as a strategy for developing fluency and confidence in early and struggling readers, and as a strategy for teaching English as a second or foreign language, particularly in East Asian countries. For teachers looking for examples of choral reading to use as models, YouTube is an invaluable resource. Go to youtube.com and search for "Choral Reading Example." A video in which five high school students present a choreographed reading of a passage from "The Tempest" is an excellent model. "Choral Readings from Drama Night" provides more examples of choreographed choral reading by a 10th-grade English class. For an example of choral speaking within an Asian school context, check out "Choral Speaking Take 2 SMKPJ," which features recitations of excerpts from, among other works, *King Lear*. Finally, spoken word poetry, when performed by two or more speakers, may also be considered an example of choral poetry and is the topic of Chapter 4; a good example can be found on YouTube under a search for "Seven Deadly Sins— Jocelyn Ng & Will Giles—Youth Speaks."

This was my attitude, too, as a middle-school language arts teacher at the School for Creative and Performing Arts (SCPA) in Cincinnati many years ago, until one day on a hunch I handed my 8th-grade, period-after-lunch, teach-me-if-you-dare class a set of Shel Silverstein poems and instructed them to form small groups of two or three, take a few minutes to rehearse, and then perform them for the class. I was a bit nervous about the assignment because although this was SCPA and several of the students were certified hams, many more struggled as readers and few in this class were academically motivated. But I figured that the poems were short and funny and the chance to rehearse and work with a friend or two would provide enough support for a moderately successful exercise.

To my surprise and delight, the students immediately understood what to do. They formed small groups, "scored" their poem by deciding which partner or partners would say what phrases or lines, and with a few minutes' practice, some overnight "fermentation," and a quick review the next day, their performances were clever and remarkably smooth. Some groups even *choreographed* their reading, and a few had rehearsed so well they were nearly able to recite their parts from memory. Our experience of choral reading echoed that of Grace Loar, a teacher who organized a choral recital of poetry for her high school classes with great success and wrote in 1932 in *English Journal* that

> Speaking poetry together gives freedom to self-conscious and timid students who could not speak alone. It improves enunciation and brings about better co-ordination of voice and body. Memorizing poetry in this way is a pleasure. Another important value of group speaking is that it is a pleasant, constructive, worth-while [sic] way to interest and direct a large number of students. (p. 715)

Just as significantly, when students are allowed to choose their partners, select from a range of poems, and decide for themselves how best to score their poem to bring out their particular interpretation of it, their attention to the structure and rhythm of poetry in relation to its meaning is fully engaged, and their capacity to read with fluency and greater comprehension is enhanced.

CHORAL READING IN THE CLASSROOM

How does choral reading look in a secondary school classroom to-day? Mr. Riordan and the 25 students in his 8th-/9th-grade English class volunteered to try it out. Appropriate grade-level poems were selected at Poets.Org (www.poets.org), the website of the Academy of American Poets, which permits users to search for and download poems on a wide range of topics and by American poets past and present. Traditional poetry anthologies that cover a wide range of topics and cultures and the poetry collections of particular authors are a vital classroom resource. But where resources are stretched or thin, the Internet can also be an invaluable tool.

Demonstration

The choral reading exercise in Mr. Riordan's class began with a demonstration. Because the *Twilight* book series and movie was the current rage, two student teachers presented a choral reading of the poem "Dracula" by Salwa Al-Neimi, which begins:

Protruding, rebelling against the lips,
the long, pointed, ill-fated fang stared at me,

To score the poem, we first underlined continuously the phrases that we wanted one or both speakers to read:

Poets.Org and the Poetry Foundation

Two of the best and most dependable sources of poetry and resources currently on the Internet are the Poetry Foundation (www.poetryfoundation.org) and Poets.Org (www.poets.org). Each of these sites provides access to hundreds if not thousands of poems written by scores of contemporary and canonical poets from both English and foreign-language (in English translation) traditions. Both sites are easy to navigate and provide powerful search tools. They also provide a range of materials for teachers, and Poets.Org has a well-developed resource for teens. There are a wide range of audio and video recordings available on both sites.

<u>Protruding, rebelling against the lips,</u>
<u>the long, pointed, ill-fated fang stared at me,</u>

Then we returned and decided which speaker, 1 or 2 or both, would say which phrase:

    BOTH   **1**   **2**
<u>Protruding, rebelling against the lips,</u>

     1   **2**   **1**   **2**   **1**
<u>the long, pointed, ill-fated fang stared at me,</u>

Then the student teachers rehearsed. Their later performance in class had the students sitting up in their desks at attention.

Whole-Class Reading

The next step was to have the students read a poem that the teachers had already half-scored. Then, we invited the class to score the second half as a group. We chose "Identity Crisis" by F. D. Reeve:

                1   **ALL**
<u>"Not to succeed in your chosen profession is</u> <u>unthinkable.</u>

      2, 3   **4**
<u>Either you make it or—you're beyond the pale.</u>

      ALL
<u>Do you understand?"</u>

   6   **2**
<u>"No," he shakes his head.</u>

        ALL
<u>"Are you ready to forage for freedom?"</u>

   6   **2**
<u>"No," he adds,</u>

         7
<u>"I mean, why is a cat always shaking his head?"</u>

Identity Crisis

by F. D. Reeve

He was urged to prepare for success: "You never can tell,
 he was told over and over; "others have made it;
 one dare not presume to predict. You never can tell.

Who's Who in America lists the order of cats
 in hunting, fishing, bird-watching, farming,
 domestic service—the dictionary order of cats

who have made it. Those not in the book are beyond the pale.
 Not to succeed in your chosen profession is unthinkable.
 Either you make it or—you're beyond the pale.

Do you understand?"
            "No," he shakes his head.
 "Are you ready to forage for freedom?"
                    "No," he adds,
 "I mean, why is a cat always shaking his head?

Because he's thinking: who am I? I am not
 only one-ninth of myself. I always am
 all of the selves I have been and will be but am not."

"The normal cat," I tell him, "soon adjusts
 to others and to changing circumstances;
 he makes his way the way he soon adjusts."

"I can't," he says, "perhaps because I'm blue,
 big-footed, lop-eared, socially awkward, impotent,
 and I drink too much, whether because I'm blue

or because I like it, who knows. I want to escape
 at five o'clock into an untouchable world
 where the top is the bottom and everyone wants to escape

from the middle, everyone, every day. I mean,
  I have visions of two green eyes rising
  out of the ocean, blinking, knowing what I mean."

"Never mind the picture, repeat after me
  the self's creed. What he tells you you
  tells me and I repeats. Now, after me:

I love myself, I wish I would live well.
  Your gift of love breaks through my self-defeat.
  All prizes are blue. No cat admits defeat.
The next time that he lives he will live well."

We assigned roles with up to ten individual speakers, and combined some individuals (depending, optimally, on voice quality), in order to have the entire class speak as a chorus. The students read through the first half of the poem easily following the demonstration and as a class were able to make interesting suggestions for scoring the second half that demonstrated their awareness of phrasing and emphasis within the poem.

Group Work

We next invited the students to group themselves into threes and fours and quickly read aloud a number of poems we had preselected from the website: "A Green Crab's Shell," by Mark Doty; "What the Angels Left," by Marie Howe; "Yellow Beak," by Stephen Dobyns; "The Adventures of a Turtle," by Russel Edson, and others. The students worked intently for the remainder of the 50-minute period, reading and rereading each line aloud as they scored it to see how it sounded aloud.

Students experimented with different scoring techniques. For example, one group of four divided the words among the speakers according to their parts of speech: the first speaker would say all the "descriptive words" (adjectives and adverbs), the second speaker all the verbs, the third all the nouns, and the fourth, all the prepositions. But after trying to read the poem this way they reconsidered, and scored their poem in the manner of the models we had presented.

All scorings done by the students showed they understood how to control the rhythm and emphasis within the poems by dividing lines into meaningful phrases and multiplying the number of voices to produce emphasis. By allotting particular words or phrases in a poem to a single speaker, they also learned how to focus attention on those words and to make the reading seem more consistent and patterned. For example, in the following scoring of "What the Angels Left" by Beth, Jan, Doug, and Charlene, the use of a chorus of voices raises the dramatic tension of the reading, while the allotment of "At first" and "Then"—the first words in the first two stanzas—to the same speaker bring consistency to the reading and help to emphasize a change in the situation. The use of single voices for longer phrases ("seemed perfectly harmless" and "I began to notice them" by the second speaker, "They lay on the kitchen table" by the third, and "in the blue light" by the fourth) gives these phrases relatively less emphasis:

> 1   ALL   2
> At first, the scissors seemed perfectly harmless.
>
>   3   4
> They lay on the kitchen table in the blue light.
>
> 1   2   ALL
> Then I began to notice them all over the house,

EXTENDING THE APPROACH:
IF WE COULD DO IT OVER AGAIN

The students in Mr. Riordan's class and the student teachers and I rated the choral reading activity a fine success, but in retrospect we could also find some room for improvement on our strategies. How might you adapt this exercise to work in your classroom?

For example, to maximize the time students had to score and rehearse their poems, we preselected a number of poems that were relatively short and clever but not controversial or emotionally intense. We thought these were poems that might appeal to a broad range of personalities and interests. One consequence was that although the students enjoyed the activity, they did not seem invested personally in the poems when they discussed why they chose a particular arrangement for the readings.

Or, a class could select a single poem, and then be challenged to score it in small, autonomous groups. This would allow for a whole-class compare and contrast exercise, and a discussion of the differences in meanings produced by each group. By comparing differences in scoring across the same poem, the different effects of scoring decisions may stand out more.

Teachers could also show students examples of choreographed choral readings from YouTube.

CHORAL READING AND POETRY IN A HIGH-STAKES WORLD

When most educators discuss the instructional merits of choral reading today they stress its benefits for improving fluency in beginning and intermediate readers in the elementary grades. For example, the Read Strong Center at The University of Texas at Austin suggests:

> Choral reading provides support for students who may ordinarily feel self-conscious or nervous about reading aloud in class. Reading along with more fluent readers enables less proficient readers to be successful with a shared text. . . . When students participate in choral reading on a regular and repeated basis, students will internalize the fluent reading of the text being read and begin to transfer their developing fluency to other texts. (http://www.edb. utexas.edu, click "Read Strong" and then "Choral Reading")

Choral reading is also promoted as a means for promoting fluency in learners of English as a second or foreign language, particularly as a means of developing fluency and accuracy in pronunciation, which may partially explain its appeal to English-language teachers and learners in Asia.

But I open this book with choral reading because of its benefits as a strategy for developing other even more important skills and practices, such as reading comprehension skills and the habit of reading *closely*—of paying attention to every word and phrase in relation to all other words or phrases in a sentence or a line of poetry and considering how each word and each mark of punctuation contributes to intended and perhaps unintended meanings. In the choral reading that is promoted by reading and ESL/EFL specialists in the United States and around the world today, the texts that students read are pre-selected and pre-scripted—and so each reader's part is also pre-determined—before the students ever see the text. This means, of course, that students in these situations are also prevented from having to look thoughtfully at every word in the text they are given to read, since it has already been done for them. They're not expected to give much thought to what a text means or, with slight variance in rhythm or emphasis, could mean; someone has already done all the thinking at that level for them.

In contrast, the choral reading activity described in this chapter is all about the development of comprehension skills through closely attending to the ways that words fit together and the ways that different scorings of a poem and different combinations and qualities of voice might produce very different readings and meanings of the same text. This approach follows the principle that the students, not the teachers, decide how the poems should be scored and read. By placing the responsibility for the meaning of the reading in the hands of the readers, we almost guaranteed that the reading would be coherent and consistent in its execution.

The approach to choral reading described in this chapter may also help serve as an antidote to the idea that reading is an act of mass consumption—an idea that is closely tied to the dominance of novels as a genre within contemporary literature and literature education and to the preoccupation with fluency as a prerequisite for comprehension that is seen in policy documents today. Fluent reading is, of course, important; but when it takes the place of or overrides the equally important ability to read slowly and carefully and to consider alternate meanings, it undermines the very outcomes it aims to promote. Choral reading of poetry, practiced once or twice a month within a language arts curriculum, may help to restore some balance or provide an alternative set of strategies for reading texts with dense, tightly organized ideas.

Paul Fleischman

One exception to the practice of having students score their own poems rather than have them scored for them may be the work of children's poet Paul Fleischman. In three children's books, *I Am Phoenix: Poems for Two Voices* (Fleischman & Nutt, 1989, HarperCollins), *Joyful Noise: Poems for Two Voices* (Fleischman & Beddows, 2004, HarperCollins), and *Big Talk: Poems for Four Voices* (Fleischman & Giacobbe, 2008, Candlewick), Fleischman and his illustrators offer dozens of original poems scored for two or four voices. Although the audience for these poems is students in the intermediate and upper elementary grades, the quality of the verse and illustrations provides an excellent series of models not simply for scoring and reading poetry chorally, but for *writing* original choral poems as well.

Finally, a word about choral reading's capacity as a practice for building literary awareness and aesthetic sensitivity. Poetry's linguistic roots and continuing attraction stem as much from its vocal as its written qualities. The way in which words are chosen and punctuated and placed on the page remains intimately tied to how a poem is meant to *sound*. When poems are spoken to an audience (even if it is only ourselves), the experience becomes communal. As a technique for awakening awareness of the basic elements and structure of poetry and for providing a sense of rhythm, particularly in free, nonrhyming verse, there is perhaps nothing more powerful than giving a group of readers a poetic text and asking them to come to some agreement about how they'd like to read it aloud as a group.

KEEP IN MIND

- Providing models or demonstrations of choral reading before the students begin to work will help to avoid confusion about what the final products and performances should look like. Providing different models with slightly different approaches will signal to students that they can be creative and vary their approaches as well.

- Depending on time and resources, you may want to provide students with a range of appropriate poems or allow them to find their own poems as a group. The more choices the students have, the more engaged and enthusiastic they are likely to be.
- Take time to allow the students to score, arrange, and rehearse their own poems. The more decisions the students have to make for themselves, the more they're likely to learn.
- Keep the entire activity playful, light, and experimental, but also find time at the end for some serious discussion/debriefing (or even writing) about the students' processes for scoring and rehearsing each poem.
- Students will learn and retain more from choral reading if multiple approaches are tried several times throughout the year rather than if they are only used once or twice.

CHAPTER 2

Skin Poetry

Figuring Out Figurative Language

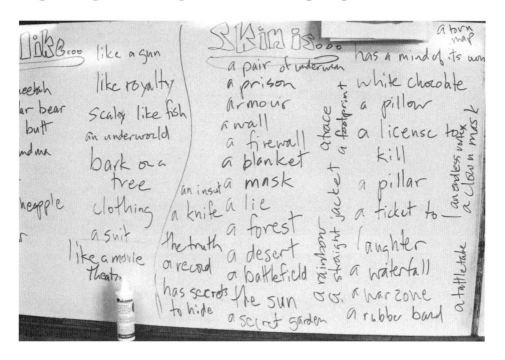

Though passion may have strained, it must not break our bonds of affection. The mystic chords of memory, stretching from every battlefield, and patriot grave, to every living heart and hearthstone, all over this broad land, will yet swell the chorus of the Union, when again touched, as surely they will be, by the better angels of our nature.

—Abraham Lincoln, First Inaugural Address

Since the advent of realism around the turn of the 20th century, the use of grand metaphors in American literature has been downplayed in favor of simple word choice; shorter, more direct sentences; and plain, vernacular turns of phrase. This shift signaled a turn away from Victorian English toward a style that seemed more democratic and populist and, it might be argued, "honest," in which words were to be used to convey meaning as directly as possible.

But now imagine how Lincoln's First Inaugural Address of 1861 might have sounded in the language of today, stripped of its figurative expressions:

> People in the northern and southern states are in conflict today, but we must not forget that we still like and depend on each other. If every person in the nation and in every home remembers the many battles and lives that have been lost to unite us in the past, we will also realize that we are still one nation. If we do not let anger control our behavior we can still work out our differences and avoid a civil war.

Comparing the two passages, I am not sure that my translation is any clearer than Lincoln's original, and most certainly it produces less feeling and does not persuade or move readers as much. Lincoln and other great writers of the 19th century understood what many of us in the 21st have learned to distrust: that language is almost unavoidably metaphorical when used well, and that a carefully chosen image fuses emotion with cognition in ways that often produce great clarity of meaning and even greater power to move listeners or readers to action and understanding.

This chapter is about reclaiming metaphors and other figures of expression as tools for clarifying the most mundane and yet critical features of our daily lives.

As a middle school language arts teacher many years ago, I had the opportunity to team-teach writing in a computer lab with an African-American colleague. One day in a conversation with another African-American teacher and me she described the enormous vocabulary that, in her childhood, she had acquired for describing skin color. I was fascinated by her story because, growing up White in an all-White community, my skin's color and texture were hardly ever a topic of conversation, and I realized that my vocabulary for talking about skin was quite limited. I was reminded of a poem I'd recently read by Nikki Giovanni in a collection of her poems, *My House* (1972), "Poem (For Nina)," which begins, "we are all imprisoned *in the castle of our skins*/ and some of us have said so be it." We decided on a lesson in poetry writing and figurative language

---

Nikki Giovanni

Nikki Giovanni's official website (nikki-giovanni.com) provides a wealth of biographical, commercial, and contact information about this famous African American's work and its influence within American letters. Giovanni was born in Knoxville, Tennessee, and grew up in Cincinnati, Ohio, with frequent summer trips back to Knoxville with her sister. Her parents were teachers and activists in the Civil Rights Movement in Cincinnati in the 1950s and 1960s. Giovanni attended Fisk University, where she met Dudley Randall and many other African-American poets of the 1960s, including Robert Hayden, Margaret Walker, and LeRoi Jones (now Amiri Baraka). After college, she returned to Cincinnati and became a force in its literary scene. When I was a teacher in Cincinnati in the 1980s, it seemed that every African-American student in my classes had a parent or a relative who knew Nikki personally from that time. But by then, she had moved on, to an M.F.A. program at Columbia University in New York, to multiple award-winning books and recordings, and eventually to a distinguished professorship at Virginia Tech University, not too far from her birthplace in Knoxville, Tennessee. Giovanni's poems and readings are available directly through her website, most independent local bookstores, through Amazon.com, Powells.com, Barnes and Noble and other online booksellers, and in MP3 version, through Rhapsody.com (www.rhapsody.com; search for Nikki Giovanni).

---

for our next writing lab session that would tap the vocabulary and consciousness of the students of color and raise the cultural awareness of the White students in our classes.

The process was simple. At the beginning of the double-period writing session, the students pulled their chairs together in front of a large piece of butcher paper we had taped to the wall that was divided into two columns: Similes (Skin is like . . .); and Metaphors (Skin is . . .). We invited the students to brainstorm, provided some examples ourselves to prime their imaginations, and we were off. At first, the ideas came slowly, and most were clichés: smooth as silk, like cream; a chocolate dessert. But then, we noticed that the students were looking at their own skin, touching their forearms, and giggling. "My skin is a forest," one student declared. "Mine is cratered like the moon," another suggested, feeling his face. "Mine is a sweet candy kiss," another whispered. "My knees are a desert,"

Poem (For Nina)

we are all imprisoned *in the castle of our skins*
and some of us have said so be it
if i am in jail my castle shall become
my rendezvous
my courtyard will bloom with hyacinths and jack-in-the-
      pulpits
my moat will not restrict me but will be filled
with dolphins sitting on lily pads and sea horses ridden by
      starfish
goldfish will make love
to Black mollies and color my world Black Gold
the vines entwining my windows will grow butterflies
and yellow jackets will buzz me to sleep
the dwarfs imprisoned will not become my clowns
for me to scorn but my dolls for me to praise and fuss
with and give tea parties to
my gnomes will spin cloth of spider web silkiness
my wounded chocolate soldiers will sit in evening coolness
or stand gloriously at attention during that midnight sun
for i would have no need of day patrol
if i am imprisoned in my skin let it be a dark world
with deep bass walking a witch doctor to me for spiritual
      consultation
let my world be defined by my skin and the skin of my
      people
for we   spirit to spirit   will embrace
this world
      12 jan 72
      Nikki Giovanni

---

one said, then laughed. Soon the metaphors and similes were flying and we struggled to record them all on the paper. In 20 minutes of fits and starts and long pauses followed by eruptions of ideas, we had collected more than 100 metaphors and similes to describe our skin.

The next step was for each student to write a poem entitled, "My Skin." We provided no examples but did suggest the poems didn't have to rhyme, and that the students could use any metaphors or similes on the paper or that came to them as they wrote. Within 25 more minutes, the students had each written a one-page poem they were eager to share. There was barely enough time at the end to put Giovanni's poem on the overhead projector, read it aloud, and have a short discussion about points of comparison and contrast between Giovanni's and the students' ideas about skin.

At our next meeting, we reviewed the assignment and returned to "Poem (For Nina)." A poem didn't have to rhyme to be good, we suggested, but it probably should have *rhythm,* or a kind of pace or beat. We looked again at Giovanni's poem, and noted that it didn't rhyme, but that the way the words were placed on the page provided readers with some directions about when to pause, when to read quickly, and when to emphasize particular words or phrases, so that the language of the poem flowed as it was read. The students wondered why some words were in italics and why Giovanni used capital letters in some places and not others, and noted the effect this left for us as readers. We asked the students to take a look at their poems and think about how they might rewrite them with more attention to details such as word placement and capitalization and punctuation. We fired up our 15 then-state-of-the-art Apple IIE computers, instructed the students to sit in pairs, and revise/rewrite their poems using word processing features as creatively as they might. A few days later we filled the hall bulletin board with the class's original, clever, and remarkably candid poems on the topic of "My Skin."

SKIN POETRY IN THE CLASSROOM

Ms. Parker's Classroom

The skin poems from those first lessons do not survive, but fortunately teachers in three project schools chose to field-test skin poetry in their classrooms. Ms. Parker's middle-school students brainstormed for much of the period on the topic of their skins. A few of their metaphors and similes were:

Skin is like . . . /Skin as . . .	Skin is . . .
bread	a starry night
a drawing board	chocolate
a quilt	a phoenix
a bumpy road	a plate
a map	a balloon
a science experiment	a diary

They wrote first drafts of their poems quickly, and following a reading and discussion of "Poem (For Nina)" the next day, they moved to the computer lab and revised their drafts using multiple fonts and other formatting features, as did Nikki Giovanni's poem. The class was racially diverse, and this was reflected in the multiple perspectives on skin within the poems. Shanna, an African-American girl, wrote:

My skin is like a bowl of chocolate the color the
texture the look the smell of it,
    . . . but when I run on the track . . . I just can't
wait to get home and get
in the shower and feel like silk and chocolate again
    My skin is beautiful

Teresa, another African-American student, wrote:

I KEEP THINGS TO MYSELF MY SKIN IS A
DIARY
I HAVE LOTS OF THINGS GOING ON UNDER
MY SKIN MY SKIN IS LIKE A STORY
MY SKIN IS ALWAYS SHINING MY SKIN IS
LIKE THE SUN

However, Alicia, who was White, never mentioned the color of her skin or its beauty, or that it was a significant part of her identity:

My skin is like a quit
It patches itself
Back together
My skin is like a map
All the lines take
You somewhere

Ms. Hendrick's Classroom

In Ms. Hendrick's class, perhaps because she and the majority of the students were African American, skin color as a marker of identity was foregrounded for White students in this classroom in a way that it wasn't in Ms. Parker's. For example, Angela, who was White, wrote that her skin was "a rainbow, with many colors," and that:

> Skin is
> The story of
> two different worlds.

Allen, who was White, described his skin as "white as glue," and "white," and "a better door than a window." During the sharing session of their drafts, comments from several African-American students about assumptions that Whites (and store clerks in particular) made about their intentions based on race led to a lively debate between Allen and the rest of the class. Allen argued that his style of clothing led many African-American students in the school to suspect he was a "narc"—and therefore that appearances were just as deceiving to Blacks as to Whites. Exchanges were heated, but the conversation remained civil and everyone's point of view was aired, largely due to Ms. Hendrick's moderating influence, as in stories she told to illustrate the ways in which African Americans and Whites sometimes misunderstand and misjudge each other.

Ms. Clinton's Classroom

Both in similarity and in contrast, the work of Ms. Clinton's rural, all-White tenth-grade class reflected the complexity and extension of metaphorical thinking that comes with age and the lack of racial consciousness about one's skin within an all-White world. Like the other two classrooms, the brainstorming process of metaphors and similes began slowly but gained creativity and speed as Ms. Clinton and I persisted, offering suggestions and pushing the students to let their imaginations "go wild."

These students' poems foregrounded issues of teenage angst and confidence mixed with a hint of gothic literariness. Alex wrote:

What is my skin
Let me ponder

                                        It is an endless vortex
                                        It brings in the unnecessary
                                        But leaves the necessary.

Brandon's poem was one of only a handful in any of the classes that rhymed:

I can never be who I want to be
But I can change the way I look
I will change the cover you see
But I'm still
        The same torn paged book

In a last example, Cassie described her skin as

A footprint in the dark
It's freckled like a cheetah
A desert storm, blowing, never giving a reason
My own safe zone
A straight jacket, restraining from what wants to be done
A mystery never to be found out

EXTENDING THE APPROACH: GETTING FIGURATIVE ACROSS THE CURRICULUM

The success of "skin" as a topic for brainstorming metaphors and writing poetry is due to at least three factors. First, skin is utterly common: Everyone has it, and when they come to think of it, everyone, regardless of the color or qualities of their own skin, has feelings about theirs and probably about other people's. Second, skin is a provocative but not taboo topic, and so it lends itself to much classroom discussion and extended thinking. Third, skin is an important, if not critical, part of society and of students' lives, and the subject of much literary activity.

With a bit of brainstorming, other topics with poems that might serve as models will come to mind, and can carry this exercise across content areas. For example, "math" is one such topic. The *Journal of*

Online Mathematics and Its Applications has an online link to an article by Joanne Growney that lists six poems with mathematical imagery and six with mathematical structure (mathdl.maa.org; search under "poetry"). Another topic is "homework," and my favorite poem on the topic is "Homework! Oh, Homework!" by Jack Prelutsky, which is available online at School-Survival.net (search for "poetry"). Another topic is "my bedroom." Google "poems about my bedroom," and multiple links, including one inspired by Robert Louis Stevenson—"My Bed Is Like a Sailing Ship," at GigglePoetry.com—can be found. Other examples are "hands" (go to Poets.org and use the search feature to find three wonderful poems on "hands") and "my sister (or brother or friend)." For this last topic, an Internet search under "poems about _____" will provide innumerable poems, but my favorite is a poem by M. S. Merwin, "My Friends," available at Poets.org (links to all these sites are also available at the website that supports this book, letspoemresources.ning.com).

Once students have brainstormed and written their own poems after a model, another way to extend the approach is to go online and search for poems by other student and amateur poets. Poem-Hunter.com offers thousands of poems by published and unpublished authors. Its search engine is also very powerful. For example, a recent search for "skin" yielded 274 poems, 86 songs, 91 quotations, and 1 singer. Another site, OpenSourceShakespeare.com, provides a concordance to the Bard's plays and other advanced search engines that display quotes of all works in which a particular word or phrase appears. One last interesting (but very commercial) site is AuthorsDen.com, which also offers a very powerful search engine.

ANOTHER APPROACH: STOP MAKING SENSE

Here is an exercise that may help stimulate students' generation of original figures of speech. It is based on a game that my 12-year-old son, Mac, invented. Mac is a great fan of gothic adolescent novels—the kind with a lone teenage protagonist who may be the only sane character in a chaotic and oppressive world. From one of them he picked up the idea of blurting out phrases that seem to make no sense, either on their own or in the context in which they are uttered. For example, Mac will open with, "chicken-noodle-soup pie," to which I respond, "televisions with underwear," to which he counters a while later, "flamingoes punching bookshelves," and I respond, "pumpkin-flavored windshields." The idea is to top the previous utterance in strangeness, to avoid relating phrases to each other, and to play the game while we're doing something else— riding in the car, usually, or eating dinner—so that a spirit of out-of-the-blueness is maintained. Mac calls the game Going Random, but I prefer Stop Making Sense, because that seems to be the goal. Of course, it's also impossible to achieve, for no sooner is a phrase uttered than an image is created in our minds, and we can't help but try to figure it out, to impose a meaning on the situation. In the end, we can't stop making sense; our only hope is to try to make sense for ourselves rather than have convention make it for us.

Imagine playing this game in a classroom, not as a formal activity but as something that runs beneath the current of the day's activities. I might begin by enlisting a few of the more anarchic students in my class as coconspirators. During a discussion of something unrelated, each might alternately raise her or his hand and say something like, "chickens on the Titanic," and I would nod, and stop to write the phrase on a corner of the board or some butcher paper. In time, other students who were not in on the game initially might begin to play; we might have to stop what we were doing and do this for a while, but in the end, our creativity would be flowing; we'd have a board full of clever, original images to talk about; and we'd have had an unforgettable lesson in the power of figurative language.

SKIN POETRY IN A HIGH-STAKES WORLD

A quick check will show that the teaching of figurative language is a bona fide part of the standards for almost any district, state, or provincial curriculum in North America. Standard 2.4 of the Ontario English Curriculum for grades 9 and 10, for example, states that students will "use appropriate stylistic devices to communicate their meaning and engage their intended audience . . . (e.g., use figurative language to evoke a particular emotion in a monologue)" (edu.gov.on.ca; search "secondary English curriculum"). Similarly, Illinois Learning Standards Goal 2.A.3.a states that middle-school students should be able to "identify and analyze a variety of literary techniques (e.g., figurative language, allusion, dialogue, description, word choice, dialect) within classical and contemporary works representing a variety of genres" (isbe.state.il.us). Finally, the benchmark description of recently revised Florida Learning Standard LA.8.2.1.3 (Grade 8 Language Arts) states that "The student will locate various literary devices (e.g., sound, meter, figurative and descriptive language), graphics, and structure and analyze how they contribute to mood and meaning in poetry" (floridastandards.org). Typically, in my experience, formal assessments ask students to distinguish between figurative and literal meanings in a text or within a multiple-choice framework, to choose the "correct" interpretation of a figure of speech within a passage. Asking students to brainstorm metaphors and similes for their skin or their homework or bedroom or any aspect of their daily lives and then write poems that explicate and extend these meanings is an activity that is clearly in alignment with standards-based curriculum policy and is also likely to be good practice for The Test.

However, I want to argue in conclusion that meeting standards or passing a test is hardly the best reason for using the skin poetry approach or otherwise encouraging the celebration of figurative language in an English Language Arts classroom. The best reason (or at least the one that appeals the most to me because it is so wonderfully ironic) is that teaching about figurative language is a rare, *authorized* opportunity to subvert the normal logic and order of things. Again and again throughout the school curriculum, students and teachers are required to conform to predetermined conventions and standards. At every turn in the school day they are asked to give clear reasons and provide evidence in support of opinions, to be predictable and to always, relentlessly demonstrate that the world and their understanding of it is rational and logical and that it always, certifiably, *makes sense*.

Learning to generate and appreciate original figures of speech— expressions that take writers or speakers and readers or listeners by surprise and push them to see the commonplace in a new way— requires just the opposite of most school practices. It requires that, at least momentarily, learners *stop* making sense, stop applying conventions, and stop trying to understand something before they've experienced it. When my son, Mac, "goes random" and says to me, "Robot strawberries," and my response is "toenails in the fireplace," or when, in the heat of a brainstorming session, a student cries out, "My skin is an endless vortex," we're fighting back *against* the vortex of rationality, *against* the idea that we're all just cogs in a linguistic wheel, even as we immediately begin to wonder to ourselves "what we meant by that." In those moments, we assert the right as human beings not to be incoherent and capricious in our thinking but to make sense of reality on our own terms, and to participate in the creative, anarchic, constantly rejuvenating history of the English language.

KEEP IN MIND

- Be persistent. Every time I have used this approach students are slow at first to begin offering metaphors and similes, but eventually the pace quickens and ideas begin to flow. It is important to be prepared for this and to have prepared some clever metaphors in advance to help model and prime the process.
- Keep the process light and playful. There is no quicker way to kill a lesson in poetry or a lesson on figurative language than to impose definitions or rules or quotas in advance of brainstorming and writing. Once the students have filled a board or a sheet of butcher paper with metaphors, then it may be interesting and useful to try to organize the ideas and begin to point out their metaphorical qualities and even teach a bit of terminology, such as which phrases are examples of oxymorons (contradictions in terms, like "my skin is an exposed mask") or of synecdoche (in which a part stands for the whole, as in "give me some skin"). But these lessons in form and structure are the outcome of clever, creative language use, not its cause or prerequisite.
- The Internet has become an indispensable source of materials and very credible knowledge about poets, their poems, and poetry as a genre. The websites listed in this chapter and elsewhere in the book barely scratch the surface of what is available. Many of the sites are extensive, and include not poems and background information about poets, but glossaries of poetic terminology, powerful search engines, and hundreds

of audio and video recordings of poets and poetry lovers reading and discussing all things poetic. And if a particular poetry website does not have what you're looking for, Google or any other search engine almost certainly will.

CHAPTER 3

Blues Poetry and Other Forms of Cultural Expression

The parody, or imitation, of a famous poem or poet's work may not only be the sincerest form of flattery, it may also be one of the best and most historic ways to understand and appreciate how form and structure contribute to a poem's meaning. As far back as 1915, Frank Chandler at the University of Cincinnati wrote in *The English Journal*:

> Only by such reproduction or expression, indeed, can I appreciate art, and my ability to reproduce imaginatively the work of others quickens both my sensitiveness to that work and my capacity for beautiful expressions of my own. (p. 285)

Traditionally, parody has been used to study classical poetic forms, such as the sonnets of Shakespeare and Petrarch. In other cases, students have copied poetic forms to "get a feel" for the style of a particular poem, such as Edward Fitzgerald's translation of *The Rubaiyat* of Omar Khayyam in Chandler's article or the poetry of Walt Whitman, Amy Lowell, or Carl Sandberg in an article by Newark, New Jersey teacher Charles Glicksberg in 1940.

In this reworking of the strategy, students study the stanza structure and rhyme scheme of forms of poetry that are endemic to specific cultures, for three purposes: to raise those forms up and give them the respect and consideration they deserve within the English curriculum; more generally, to serve as a culturally relevant exercise in the basics of structural analysis; and as an outlet for students for the emotions and ideas those forms were created to express.

I was not a student of the blues before trying this approach with students for the first time at the School for Creative and Performing Arts. I was looking for texts that were, in those pre-Internet days, "multimodal," meaning texts that would lend themselves not just to reading and writing but also to performance and perhaps some sort of visual arts activities. I came upon a poem by Langston Hughes, "Po' Boy Blues," in an anthology of African-American poetry and stopped, realizing for the first time that the blues, which I had always thought of as music, were also a form of poetry. Reading through the poem, I immediately recognized the regularity of the rhyme and stanza scheme, and remembered other blues songs with the same pattern. I headed off to the blues section of a local music store and purchased several cassette tapes of Billie Holiday, Leroy Carr, and a collection of recordings by classic Mississippi delta blues artists and then sat down to listen.

I learned that the blues did not consist of the single form of Hughes's poem but of many different rhyme schemes and variations, although Hughes's poem appeared to have the most common pattern. I made the decision to keep my approach simple, at least at the beginning, and to focus on teaching students this one pattern, using multiple examples. I transcribed two more songs, one by Billie Holiday, "Stormy Blues," and one by Leroy Carr, "Midnight Hour Blues"; made an overhead for presentation, and prewound my cassette tapes. The next morning, as my first period, it's-too-early-I-just-want-to-sleep 8th-grade class stumbled in, Billie Holiday was playing on my boom box. "Hey," an African-American student announced to the class, "That's the music my parents listen

What Are the Blues?

- Although elements can be traced to musical traditions in West Africa and to African-American culture from slavery through the Reconstruction period in the rural U.S. South, the blues that we know today were named in the late 19th or early 20th centuries. The form did not become well-known nationally until the Great Migration of the early 1930s and 1940s.

- The term "the blues" comes from the phrase "the blue devils," which meant to be depressed or held involuntarily in a state of deep melancholy.

- The invention/discovery of the blues marks a turning point in African- American music. Instead of one person "calling" in song and another singer or group calling back as in a spiritual or secular "field hollering," in the blues an individual singer calls in one line, repeats the call (often with slight variation), and then answers herself or himself with an ironic response. This reflects the shift in performance venue for the blues, from church or field to juke joint and later, to the nightclub.

- The first blues recording, "Laughing Song," was made in 1895 by George W. Johnson. The African-American composer W. C. Handy first heard the blues while waiting for a train in Mississippi in 1903. He helped popularize the song form with the publication of several musical compositions between 1911 and 1914.

- The blues as a written poetic form originated during the Harlem Renaissance in the 1920s and 1930s, when Langston Hughes, Sterling Brown, and James Weldon Johnson "formalized" the blues by rewriting its three single-line lyrics as a three-couplet stanza with the rhyme scheme ABABCB.

to!" Her comment launched a quick discussion in which students tried to name the singer, talked about other musicians their parents listened to, and then to a brief introductory lesson on the blues. With the overhead on the projector, we outlined the rhyme scheme in Hughes's poem and the stanza format of two repeated couplets and a third that completed the idea of the first two:

I was a good boy,	A
Never done no wrong.	B
Yes, I was a good boy,	A
Never done no wrong.	B
But this world is weary	C
An' de road is hard an' long.	B

"Now, listen," I said, and quickly played my recordings of Holiday and Carr, noting the similarity of their blues poems to Hughes's poem.

And then, gathering up my courage, I *sang* Hughes's poem to the class. Now, I am not a gifted singer and I have absolutely no musical talent, but I did my best to imitate the raspy bass of Louis Armstrong or James Brown, and to "accompany" myself at the end of each stanza by mimicking the strum of a bass guitar: duh-Duh-duh-duh, duh-Duh-duh-duh, duh-Duh-duh-DUH-DUH! My students were shocked at my behavior that early in the morning, but then they began to laugh and accompany me, pounding out a beat on their desks and taking up their own guitar rifts at the end of each stanza. Out of breath and completely hoarse, I had a quick discussion about the meaning of each poem and what the blues were about. The blues, the students decided, were about *complaining*. Only in each case it didn't seem like it was just complaining; the poems were also about surviving and not giving in, and how their struggles made the singer stronger.

"Okay," I told the class, "now here's what we're going to do: We're going to write 'The SCPA Blues.' Yes, write a blues poem using the ABABCB rhyme scheme and stanza format about something at SCPA you want to complain about." The students loved the school, but it took them no time to come up with a list of things—the cafeteria, rehearsals, riding the bus, particular rules (and some classes)—that lent themselves to the blues. The students went to work, writing, rehearsing, and then, by the end of a single 50-minute period, performing (I closed the door) their poems.

The final poems and their performance were raucous. I had originally hoped to publish them in a bulletin board display entitled, "The SCPA Blues," but the topic and directness of some of the lines led me to decide otherwise. For the most part, the students adhered to the rhyme scheme and stanza format of the blues, with some departures in the length of individual lines that became apparent as they sang. On the one hand, I wondered what Pandora's box I had opened in allowing the students to voice their complaints about aspects of the school program within my classroom. But on the other hand, I marveled at the release this seemed to provide to the students and at their total engagement with the assignment. Over the years, whenever I have used this same approach, be it in a middle-school or high-school class, in an undergraduate teacher education program, or when the students in my teacher education classes have tried it in their field placements, it has never failed—either as a strategy for introducing the structural features of poetic forms or as a cathartic experience for the students. In the end, I have concluded that whatever problems are aired are typically already shared knowledge, and that in not publishing the poems or sharing them outside of class no harm is done and the dignity of the institution and individuals is preserved.

WATCHING, WRITING, AND SINGING THE BLUES IN THE CLASSROOM

To field-test this approach, we made a number of adjustments and updates from the way I had taught blues poetry 20 years before. First, students wrote their poems in small groups rather than individually. Second, we decided to take advantage of video versions of blues songs and poetry available on YouTube (youtube.com), rather than play audio recordings of blues singers and musicians. And third, one of the student teachers was an accomplished guitarist, so we borrowed his talents to accompany performances. YouTube is an extraordinary resource for teaching. A quick search of keywords such as "Billie Holiday," "Billie Holiday Stormy Blues," "Langston Hughes Blues," "Leroy Carr," or a wide range of other keywords and search terms yields hundreds, if not thousands, of short videos with relatively high resolution for download. None of the three classrooms in our field test were equipped with permanent LCD projectors or laptops. In the end, with a bit of preparation and using a combination of portable projectors, our own laptops, and some portable speakers, we were able to show YouTube video clips in all three classrooms with few, if any, glitches (again, links to all the websites featured in this chapter are available at letspoemresources.ning.com).

Unfortunately, however, even if classrooms have live Internet connections, many school districts' filters prevent teachers or students from accessing YouTube or downloading videos from the site. This was also the case in several of the schools where we field-tested blues poetry. Our solution was to download and save the videos we wanted to show at home or away from the schools and then play them in the classrooms as video files using a video player like Windows Media, QuickTime, or RealPlayer. To download the videos, we used the service provided free by an online site, Zamzar.com. At Zamzar, we clicked the tab marked "Download Video," copied the URL from the YouTube video we wanted to download, selected the file format we wanted (mpg or wmv work well for Windows Media; mov works well for QuickTime; and RealPlayer will play all of these, in my experience), added our e-mail address in step three, and then clicked step four (convert). Within 24 hours, Zamzar sends a message to the e-mail address with a link to a site where the video can be downloaded as a file. From there, the video can be copied to a CD, DVD, or any storage device.

To introduce the approach, we began by alternately playing the videos and asking for input from the students about whether they had heard of the blues before, what the blues were about, and if they knew any famous blues singers. We distributed a one-page handout with the lyrics to "Po' Boy Blues," by Langston Hughes, "Stormy Blues," by Billie Holiday, and "Midnight Hour Blues," by Leroy Carr. Rather than tell the students what the rhyme scheme and stanza format were, we worked with the students to describe these inductively by having them compare and contrast the structure of the rhyme and stanzas across the three poems. As the students noted similarities across the three poems, we made notes on an overhead of the same handout and had the students copy these notes on their handouts. Finally, to give the students a clear idea of what their performance would look like, we sang "Po' Boy Blues," accompanying ourselves by drumming on a desk and vocalizing (or, in the case of one talented student teacher, playing) guitar rifts between lines and stanzas.

Ms. Lewis's Classroom

In Ms. Lewis's classroom, the activity lasted 2 days. On the first day, the students were surprised and then delighted when they

Online Blues Resources

The quality and quantity of online resources that are available to teachers who are interested in teaching their students about the blues as both a musical and poetic form is vast. My advice is to search for "the blues" and "blues poetry" online and then browse liberally and for a long time. Here, in my searches, are five of the best developed and most interesting sites; all can be accessed at letspoemresources.ning.com:

1. *YouTube.* As a source of music and performance of classic and current blues music, YouTube sets a high standard. Search for blues under artists such as Billie Holiday, Bessie Smith, Langston Hughes, as well as the title of blues songs and poems: "Weary Blues," "Stormy Blues," "Midnight Hour Blues," and even "Funeral Blues" by the British poet W. H. Auden.

2. *PBS.Org.* The Public Broadcasting Service offers an extensive site on "The Blues" (www.pbs.org/theblues), which includes pages with a series of lesson plans and an excellent list of links to other sites (click on "Partners").

3. *Edsitement.* The National Endowment for the Humanities (edsitement.neh.gov) offers a site on "Forms of Poetry" that pays special homage to Langston Hughes and the blues poetry form and also includes lesson plans. This site also links to the Poetry.org site, and its excellent resources on the blues and several noted blues poets.

4. *Smithsonian Education.* If you're looking for examples of how other teachers have taught blues poetry and some examples of poems their students have written, try "The Music in Poetry" site at the Smithsonian online site (smithsonianeducation.org).

5. *History sites.* An interesting project for students might be to research multiple historical accounts of the development of the blues and "triangulate" (compare and contrast) historical accounts. Three interesting (and sometimes slightly contradictory) sites are "A Brief History of the Blues" at AllAboutJazz.com, Wikipedia (wikipedia.org; search for "Blues"); and TheBlueHighway.com, an archive of photos and short bios on classic and contemporary blues artists.

learned they were going to write about life at their high school. A few students chose to work individually, but most quickly fell into groups of two or three and spent the remaining half of the period brainstorming topics and working on rhymes. One of the advantages of working with small groups was that we were able to circulate in the room quickly and help as the groups initially worked to master the ABABCB rhyme scheme of their first stanza and to tighten some lines—that is, to reduce the number of syllables in a line to five or six without sacrificing meaning. On day two students made some quick revisions, rehearsed their parts a bit, and then performed to the accompaniment of their classmates. Each performance was videotaped and played back to the students at the end of class, to howls of laughter and applause.

Topics for the poems ranged from boring classes to the state of the restrooms and run-ins with deans of discipline. Some of the verses expressed serious frustration, but many more were witty laments. Hillary, for example, wrote about her unrequited lunchtime hunger:

> The clock is tickin'
> It's about lunchtime . . .
> . . . My tummy is growlin'
> And I'm running out of time.

Ashley expressed some frustration with her peers in one particular class:

> The teachers need to wake up
> And handle them teens . . .
> . . . Behavior is so bad
> I'm gonna rip my jeans.

And Belinda complained about her desk:

> I hate my desk
> It's way too small . . .
> . . . I hate my desk
> It makes me feel small.

Mr. Riordan's Classroom

In Mr. Riordan's class, the poems were more focused on a single topic—a research paper for a class that apparently had been assigned with some very strict guidelines and with instructions that the research sources must be "cutting edge":

> I hate all these note cards
> Thirty minutes a night . . .
> . . . Staring at the computer
> Think I'm losing my sight.

And in the final verse:

> What's the point of this paper?
> Cutting edge's the worst . . .
> . . . When will we be done?
> This assignment's a curse.

Three students, however, chose to write a blues poem about being "forced" to have the blues:

> They made me get these blues,
> But I don't want them anymore.
> Yeah, they made me get these blues,
> But I just don't want them anymore.
> Will my grade just start hurtin'
> If I don't got the blues no more?

Afterward, Jeff, the student teacher who accompanied the students on his guitar, noted about this last group that

> They showed us that ultimately, as educators ourselves,
> we too were a part of the structure we were encouraging
> them to creatively complain about or critique. They
> learned the poetic structure and history of blues, but they
> also displayed an intuition of the less tangible "sass" and
> critical attitude that accompany the blues.

Ms. Clinton's Classroom

In Ms. Clinton's tenth-grade class another theme prevailed—that of girl-boy relations. To the tune of the student teacher's guitar, Pam wrote and then sang:

> Boys are lame,
> They drive me up the *wall* . . .
> . . . They have no game
> I hope they fall.

To which Al replied,

> Girls are so dramatic
> They always complain . . .
> . . . You can't understand them
> They can't ever contain.

Not all relations were so contentious, however. Cathy and Brad teamed to write the story of (Brad's) unrequited love:

> From the restroom I emerged
> She's shining in hallway light . . .
> . . . Gotta find out her name
> Have her in my sights.

But in the next stanza:

> Can't have her, tho'
> She says, "You're not my type"
> . . . But I'm gonna try
> Even tho' it's givin' me all this strife.

Lessons from Three Classrooms

As a teacher, the experience of these three classes taught me two lessons. The first is how sensitive each class was to the slightest suggestion and to the mood of the group as a whole. We followed the same protocol with each classroom and gave each class the same instructions, yet in each case different themes were picked up. In the case of Mr. Riordan's class, most groups chose to express their frustration with a current assignment. In Ms. Clinton's class, a brief conversation among the students led to four of five groups writing about love, not high school, as we had originally suggested. Only in Mrs. Lewis's class did the students take up the suggestion that they might write about a range of issues at their school. This indicates the authenticity of the sentiments expressed.

The second lesson I learned is about the importance of the models that we provided before the writing, which seem to have been far more critical to the students' success than our directions or even our coaching to help the students remain true to the rhyme scheme and format. We were very surprised at how quickly all the students, many of whom were from cultural backgrounds very distant from the blues, picked up the diction, or habits of speech, of blues lyrics in their writing. Words and spellings like "gotta," and "gonna," and phrases like "handle them teens" abounded in the poems of all three classrooms. One group of students in Mr. Riordan's class self-consciously drew from the first lines of "Stormy Blues" sung by Billie Holiday, "I've been down so long/Down don't worry me," and wrote, "I've been tired so long/Tired don't worry me." They also copied the variation of the stanza form that is the third verse of the song, with a reference to "Vault," an "energy" drink:

> I lose my sleep,
> I lose my head,
> I lose my grades!
> I cannot get out of bed.
> I need some Vault
> Need you bad as can be
> I've been tired so long,
> Don't hurry me.

Of course, we are also sure that most of the students had heard of and listened to the blues before we taught these lessons. But we doubt if they had ever consciously studied the form before, and we are certain that without clear models and some live performance beforehand to set expectations and provide a holistic sense of the exercise, the teaching and learning would not have been nearly as successful.

EXTENDING THE APPROACH:
THE CORRIDO AND OTHER CULTURAL FORMS

Although the blues poem is likely the most widespread and well-known modern form of poetry with folk origins—that is, to have come from popular, rather than academic or "high" culture, like the sonnet—it is far from unique. Many cultural groups, and particularly those from Latin America, the Caribbean, and East and South Asia, have developed a wide variety of forms that students from those areas and elsewhere might be interested in learning about and imitating. Within a North American context, the *corrido,* a romantic ballad form that originated in Spain and developed into a subversive way of spreading news along the U.S.-Mexican border in pre-radio and television years, remains the best-known Latina/o form of sung poetry.

Unlike the blues form, the corrido is longer and has a less regular rhyme scheme and stanza format. It consists of three parts that hearken back to the minstrelsy of medieval Europe and underscore its informational purpose: (1) a greeting and introduction from the singer/author; (2) the story itself, usually of a hero struggling against oppression; and (3) a concluding moral or lesson. Wikipedia.org reports that originally the corrido was sung to the rhythm of a waltz, although more recently in its adoption by *conjunto* bands, which follow more of a polka rhythm (for an excellent introduction, go to lib.utexas.edu/benson/border).

The best known and most studied and performed corrido today is "The Ballad of Gregorio Cortez." At the turn of the last century, Cortez was a farmer living near Austin, Texas. He was falsely accused of stealing a horse by a local (White) sheriff, and in an ensuing gunfight that was triggered by a mistranslation from English into Spanish, he shot and killed the sheriff after the sheriff had shot and killed his brother. Cortez fled and managed to evade capture by a posse of more than 300 men over a 10-day chase across South Texas. He was eventually captured, sent to prison, acquitted and then tried again, and was finally pardoned by the governor of Texas. In a period of history marked by extreme racism and tension between the Anglo government and the Mexican-American population of the region, Gregorio Cortez became a folk hero and his exploits and eventual triumph served as a model of resistance to Anglo cultural and political domination. In 1958, the noted scholar of Mexican-

American studies, Américo Paredes, published *"With His Pistol in His Hand": A Border Ballad and Its Hero,* which later became the basis of a popular television movie, *The Ballad of Gregorio Cortez,* starring Edward James Olmos, in 1982.

A full discussion of the corrido's format and teaching possibilities is beyond the scope of this chapter. However, Arts Edge, a division of The Kennedy Center (artsedge.kennedy-center.org) provides an excellent online site that includes lesson plans and English and Spanish lyrics to "The Ballad of Gregorio Cortez." In addition, the University of Arizona Poetry Center sponsors a yearly competition among Arizona high school students for original corridos. Its website (see poetrycenter.arizona.edu; search for "corrido") provides numerous links and copies of winning students' corridos. These sites, however, provide only the barest introduction to what is available online, both in terms of information and examples of the corrido. My advice is simply to conduct an Internet search for "corrido" and explore what is available.

In the English-speaking Caribbean, the most popular form of folk poetry by far is *dub poetry*, a form that originated in Jamaica in the early 1970s and has since spread to Toronto, Canada, Great Britain, and throughout many African nations that were formerly British colonies, until today it is an authentically global, pan-African phenomenon. It is a spoken form of poetry, typically accompanied by a reggae-style beat or melody written expressly for a particular poem. Like spoken word or slam poetry, dub poetry is often of a political nature and focuses on issues of social justice, but its tone is more ironic and usually less directly personal than spoken word or slam poetry. Like the corrido, dub poetry does not consist of a single or even dominant rhyme scheme and stanza format; it needs to be listened to and its rhythms and stylistics "picked up." It cannot (or at least should not) be learned as a poetic formula. As of this writing, online resources for dub poetry are less extensive than for blues poetry or the corrido, but there are many excellent clips available on YouTube (or, as an alternative, search "dub poetry" on MetaCafe.com). Another excellent site where you can listen to the work of several leading dub poets, such as Linton Kwesi Johnson, Mutabaruka, and Benjamin Zephaniah, is Last.Fm.

Teachers who are interested in introducing students to Asian poetic forms are already likely to be familiar with the Japanese *haiku* form (but if not, see the How-to-Write-a-Haiku instructions at wikiHow.com [search for "haiku"]). As a variation, try the Korean *sijo*, a three-line poem like the haiku but with longer, 14–16 syllable lines (thewordshop.tripod.com). Other Asian poetic forms and examples are available at the website Poets.org, where brief introductions and English-language examples of five forms, the *haiku, tanka,* and *renga,* from Japan; the *pantoum,* from Malaysia; and the *ghazal,* which originated in Arabia in the 7th century but later spread to Persia and Northern India, are provided. These are not folk forms, as are the blues, the corrido, and dub poetry, but they are very teachable, and their interesting patterns and connection to the cultures of Asian-American and immigrant students make them highly relevant.

For a very brief but extensive introduction to multiple poetic forms, I recommend two sites. One, devoted largely but not exclusively to Asian forms, is available at thewordshop.tripod.com (click on "home") and includes a general glossary of poetic terms as well as links to other sites explaining how to write in multiple formats, from the ode to the limerick to the Burmese climbing rhyme. An even more extensive site is "A Guide to Verse Forms" (volecentral. co.uk/vf), which aims to eventually become comprehensive in its listing and description of verse forms written in English. Again, all of these sites are linked at letspoemresources.ning.com.

TEACHING POETIC STRUCTURE IN A HIGH-STAKES WORLD

Whenever teachers and students study the structure and purpose of a genre or a specific form of writing through a combination of analysis and imitation, the learning is bound to be powerful and to extend to the learning of other forms of writing. Studying and writing about the blues or the corrido or any other culturally specific poetic form is not only an exercise in appreciating the literary heritage of a culture and its transcultural relevance; it is also an exercise in textual analysis and in learning how to write within a specific genre or format. Jeff, one of the student teachers who worked with Ms. Clinton's and Mr. Riordan's classes, remarked afterward:

Although I understood most of what I was doing in the classroom and my purposes, I never stopped to really reflect on the fact that so many different things are being accomplished with these lessons at the same time that the students are remaining very engaged and excited. Students are learning about poetry and the blues, but they're also learning so many valuable lessons about art: imitation, innovation, collective voices listening to each other and responding.

Studying the blues and other poetic forms is an exercise that aligns well with the content standards of many states and provinces. California English Language Arts Standard 3.5 for grade 6, for example, states that students will "Define how tone or meaning is conveyed in poetry through word choice, figurative language, sentence structure, line length, punctuation, rhythm, repetition, and rhyme." Grade 8 Standard 3.2 (Structural Features of Literature) states that students will "Determine and articulate the relationship between the purposes and characteristics of different forms of poetry." Similarly, Illinois State Board of Education Goal Two (Read and understand literature representative of various societies, eras, and ideas) and Standard 2.B.4b for early high school states that students will "analyze form, content, purpose, and major themes of American literature and literature of other countries in their historical perspective." Finally, British Columbia's Grade Eight Prescribed Learning Outcome (PLO) B12 states, "It is expected that students will recognize and explain how *structures* and *features of text* shape readers' and viewers' construction of meaning." That province's PLO C6 for "Writing and Representing" and its Suggested Achievement Indicator states that students should "consult a variety of texts for ideas and information and as models" and "use models to assist in understanding form and features" when writing.

However, as vital as learning how to analyze and then write within the form and features of a particular genre is, it is also extremely important not to introduce or teach form and structure in a prescriptive or formulaic way. I nearly destroyed the experience and the learning for my students the first time I taught blues poetry. Some students' lines were longer than the five syllables of Hughes's poem. I insisted that they shorten them, without taking the time to explain or to help them to see for themselves how a line with eight or nine or ten syllables could not be sung within the blues format, or how by playing with word choice or editing they could construct a tighter and more clever verse. Thinking back, I wish I had extended the lesson and provided further models and perhaps some whole-class revision activities that would have shown the students how, in poetry as in most forms of writing and good design, form follows function. In other words, I wish I had taken the time to have students read more blues poems and to discuss the ways in which structures develop not to dictate or entrap but to *enable* the expression and communication of ideas.

KEEP IN MIND

- One of the hardest things about teaching forms of writing is to avoid the urge to be formulaic or prescriptive—that is, to give students lists of abstract rules ("the rhyme scheme must be ABABCB") and expect them to follow them. Using models and having students inductively figure out "the rules" through some comparative analysis may seem to take longer and be more difficult in the short run, but has major long-term benefits in terms of students' learning and engagement with learning to write within the form and features of a genre.
- Learning to write within the structure of a particular poetic form can be challenging for students and difficult for one teacher to manage within a class of 25 or so students. In our experience, working from a whole-class demonstration and discussion format and then moving into small-group writing, at least initially, and then, once students have internalized the form somewhat, into writing in pairs or individually, helps the writing and performance process a great deal, especially in the early stages of the activity.
- Providing models not only of written poetic texts but of the reading and performance of those texts is critical. All poetry, and particularly the forms and activities described in this chapter, is fundamentally about speaking and listening first and writing and reading

later on. Video clips and audio recordings in this case are not optional in teaching students to analyze, write, and sing the blues; they are a necessity. And, as awful a singer as I am, in my experience, every time I "let my hair down" and demonstrate the blues in my classes, I find that it immediately breaks the ice and signals to the students that it's okay for them to "let their hair down," too.

CHAPTER 4

Hip-Hop and Spoken Word

The Elements of Poetry

Among all the approaches described in this book, none is
more linguistically complex, more comprehensive in its
use of poetic elements, or more popular with students
across race, class, language, and gender than hip-hop and rap, or
as it is more commonly known within community and educational
organizations, spoken word or slam poetry. In urban settings across
the world, from New York to Kayenta, Arizona, to Beijing, Mumbai,
Johannesburg, Casablanca, and Paris—in fact, almost anywhere in
the world youth are engaged creatively and politically, and disaf-
fected in some way—hip-hop has become a primary platform for
performance and social action through song.

But it is also the case that no approach described in this book
is likely to be more challenging for teachers than hip-hop poetry,

Hip-Hop as a Global Phenomenon

Hip-hop is easily the most widespread youth cultural phenomenon in the world today. Google "global hip-hop" and a range of news articles about the spread of hip-hop to France, Ghana, Korea, Iran, and even within Orthodox Jewish communities can be accessed. For a real sense of the adaptability of hip-hop to almost any language and cultural paradigm, go to YouTube and search "hip-hop" in Russia, Brazil, India, Australia, Colombia, Iran, Morocco, or subcultures in those nations (try "hip-hop Navajo," for example, or "hip-hop Berber," a group from North Africa) for a series of incredible musical treats.

Some critics may argue that hip-hop operates as the ultimate cultural homogenizer, in which the traditional forms and diversity of indigenous musical traditions are abandoned for the stylistics of urban America, but I disagree. Global hip-hop has emerged as a new genre that may adapt a Western style but incorporates older ones. For youth in parts of the world that are already culturally marginalized by U.S. commercialism, making videos in indigenous languages and broadcasting them on the Internet expands their audiences and serves as a counterpoint to the media dominance of Anglophone North America. For some lively and extended discussions of hip-hop as a global cultural phenomenon and its relation to U.S. commercialism, visit Afropop.org and search "hip-hop."

for two reasons. First, hip-hop has a bad rap among parents, colleagues, administrators, and the press. The identification of many major commercial rap artists with a "gangsta rap" lifestyle, which includes references to drug trafficking, abuse of women, violence, and extreme profanity in their lyrics combined with a very loud, aggressive, in-your-face attitude toward authority and middle-class values is likely to be the image that first comes to the minds of a school's community members, including its students, when the idea of writing hip-hop poetry is mentioned. In at least one of the two classrooms where we field-tested the approach, that image and its lyrical style were clearly what students intended to produce when we first introduced the topic. It took several video examples of hip-hop performances that were not of the gangsta variety and some firm guidelines from the teacher before the students could begin to rethink hip-hop/spoken word as a peace-loving means to express powerful emotions and ideas in ways that affirmed the best of their values.

The second challenge teachers are likely to face has to do with the poetic complexity of the form and, ironically, its popularity. Because of its ubiquity in youth culture, many students are likely to assume that they already know everything there is to be known about hip-hop as a poetic form. In fact, in both classes we worked with, there were several students who self-identified as rappers and had already taken stage names and made demo tapes. We applauded their initiative and their serious interest in writing, publishing, and performing. But we were also faced with the challenge of working with these and all the students in the class to push themselves beyond palely imitating Kanye West or Lil' Kim or Gnarls Barkley,

Hip-Hop for Social Justice: Youth Organizations

Youth Speaks is a San Francisco-based organization that focuses on working with urban teenage youth. Its website (youthspeaks.org) is one of the most comprehensive online sources of ideas and of video performances, through a special link with YouTube. This is also the organization that is featured in the annual Brave New Voices slam competition that is sponsored and broadcast by HBO.

Urban Word NYC is a New York-based organization that offers workshops and poetry events in the New York area, but is also interested in affiliations with schools and other organizations around the country. Its website is urbanwordnyc.org.

Young Chicago Authors is a Chicago-based organization whose website offers resources for teachers who are interested in bringing spoken word into their classrooms and schools. Its website is youngchicagoauthors.org.

Youth Music Exchange is an organization founded by two music educators, Drs. Michael Bitz and Bill McKinney. The site features recordings from students in New York and Indianapolis elementary, middle, and high schools of amazing musical and thematic diversity. This site is a must-visit for teachers interested in having students record some of their poems. Its website is youthmusicexchange.org.

Many other North American cities are also the sites for spoken word organizations for youth, including Seattle, Tulsa, Minneapolis, and Detroit. Search "spoken word youth organizations" and your city to locate these resources online.

both in terms of themes and in their invention of complex rhymes and creative, original metaphors. In other words, teachers are likely to find that whereas their students may be content to assume the *persona* of rappers, they will need to find opportunities and ways to push them to think and write within the genre as skilled wordsmiths—that is, as true hip-hop *poets*.

THE POETICS OF HIP-HOP AND SPOKEN WORD

Hip-hop developed in the Bronx in the early 1970s as an extension of block parties, in which DJs (or "MCs") improvised spoken rhymes over and between the playing of multiple LPs, in a style known as "remixing" or "scratching" (because the turntable of the LP was often moved in reverse and forward by the DJ, as though it were itself a musical instrument). An early stylistic influence, due to the city's large Jamaican and Caribbean population, was dub poetry (see Chapter 3), in which a poetic recital was overlaid with instrumental reggae accompaniment. New York DJs began to substitute R&B, soul, rock, and later disco music instead of reggae, and quickly expanded their roles from mediators or orchestrators of music to artists and producers in their own right, who wrote their own lyrics and mixed music and beats of their own creation with published songs.

While hip-hop was growing into a commercial mass-market medium, it was also developing as a form of urban social commentary and action through the organization of slam poetry competitions (the first National Poetry Slam was in 1990 in San Francisco; see poetryslam.com) and youth-oriented spoken word groups. This branch of the hip-hop movement appropriated much of the style and rhythm of hip-hop lyrics, but it downplayed the use of instrumental backgrounds and emphasized a populist, every-youth-is-a-poet approach. Like commercial hip-hop, the central feature of spoken word is an individual or group of individuals, each of whom speaks from her or his heart directly to a (presumably) live audience to give a very personal, first-person account of a situation or an event. There is a "soap box" quality to the communicative context of spoken word; the speaker's primary frame of reference is always clearly her or his life experience, which also grounds all of the speaker's claims, or arguments.

Although in spoken word and hip-hop the poet almost always speaks in a rapid, staccato, 4/4 beat (sometimes punctuated, for emphasis, by statements spoken without a beat), the range of poetic devices, including rhyme patterns, metaphors, and allusions, is quite wide, and provides an excellent introduction to nearly all the basic poetic devices of traditional English-language poetry. In my research, the best (and, I would argue, a nearly indispensable) source of information about the structure of hip-hop and spoken word poetry is to be found at Flocabulary.com, a small commercial company that focuses on teaching basic school subjects through rap and hip-hop media. Although neither I nor the publisher of this book can endorse Flocabulary's claims with respect to using hip-hop to teach basic school content in social studies, math, science, or even literature, the resources provided on the site for teaching the elements of hip-hop as a poetic form are excellent. In particular, I recommend the musical back beats provided on the site (click on "Hip-Hop" on the main page and then "Beats and More" on the next page for 20 different beats that can be ordered as a CD or played directly from a computer for free), and *The Rapper's Handbook* (Escher, 2006), which can either be downloaded electronically or ordered in hard copy.

The Rapper's Handbook is the most clearly organized and written handbook available on the structure and poetics of rap, and includes six chapters focusing on many different aspects of rap culture, including freestyling (rapping without a written text), performing, battling (in which two or more rappers confront one another in a battle of wits and words), recording, and motivation. The most critical part of the book for a teacher, however, may be Part (Chapter) 2, "Elevating Your Rhymes," which lays out very clearly seven basic poetic elements: slant rhymes, rhyme scheme, in-rhymes, multies, wordplay, metaphors, and vocabulary.

Slant rhyme is a term that is also used in conventional English poetics. It refers to rhymes that are not "perfect," as when the final vowel and consonant sound in two different words are identical, as in harass/morass (the hound's cry may harass/its prey into a morass)—but that may sound similar or *look* like they should rhyme, as in chorus/hoarse (they sang in a chorus/until they were hoarse) or gate/agate (please close the gate/with the look of agate). An example from hip-hop is this slant rhyme, in "Storm Coming," by Gnarls Barkley:

I could paint a picture with a pen
But a song will only scratch the skin.

It might seem at first that the use of slant rhyme would mark a poet as lazy or unable to find a rhyme for a word, or simply desperate, but in fact slant rhyme is a technique that was used by many very accomplished canonical poets, including Emily Dickinson and William Butler Yeats. Its purpose, in the hands of an accomplished rapper/poet, is to "throw" readers slightly off-balance and make them think about and look at a line of poetry a bit more closely so that the reading and the association of sound and meaning become more conscious.

Hip-hop and spoken word poetry also makes complex use of *rhyme schemes*, or patterns of rhyme that come only at the end of each line, as in this example (with my apologies in advance):

You say you think my rhymes are *lame*
But I'm tellin' ya, it's all a part of my hip-hop *game*
Before you know it, everyone will know my *name*
These lyrics will be drivin' all you cats *insane.*

In this example, the only rhyme comes at the end of each line, and would be traditionally marked AAAA. The first three rhymes are perfect and the fourth is an example of slant rhyme, because the *n* in "insane" does not perfectly match the *m* in the first three rhymes.

But rhyme scheme within hip-hop and spoken word poetry is typically far more complex and does not depend solely on end-rhyme, or rhymes that fall at the end of a line. Most rappers also make extensive use of *in-rhyme* (or, within conventional terminology, *internal rhyme*), in which words within a line of poetry rhyme, or one internal word rhymes with the end word of a line, as in this revised example of the previous poem:

You *claim* that people say my rhymes are *lame*
But I'm tellin' ya, it's all a part of my hip-hop *game*
Before you *know it*, I'll be hailed a *poet*
And everyone will know my *name*
Then my *lyrics* will drive all the *critics insane.*

Rhyming becomes even more complex in hip-hop and spoken word, and rises almost to the level of an art form by itself when rappers turn to the use of multisyllabic rhymes, or *multies.* As Escher (2006) puts it, "Multies are hallmarks of all the dopest flows, and all the best rappers use them" (p. 38). However, they are not as difficult to produce as it may seem. For example, take the first line above:

You claim that people say my rhymes are lame

In this case, I've decided that the next line should end with a multie for "rhymes are lame." This means I need to find words that rhyme with or approximate the sound of the three syllables. "Lame," I think, should be easy to rhyme, but I'm not so sure about "rhymes"—times? crimes? limes? My advice (and Escher's) is to go to a rhyming dictionary. There are several very good online resources for this, including rhymer.com and rhymezone.com, which also offers multisyllabic rhymes. In my case, I used rhymer.com and came up with "enzymes." Among the 20 alternatives listed, this word caught my imagination because an enzyme is a catalyst: it makes things happen, like . . . *fame*, which of course rhymes with "lame":

You claim that people say my *rhymes are lame,*
But you're wrong, they're my secret *enzymes for fame*

Okay, groaning if not stoning for my pathetic poetic droning is permitted here, but I hope you get my point: If I can work out a complicated rhyme scheme in a few minutes of messing around with some lines of bad poetry and a rhyming dictionary, so can any teacher or any group of relatively motivated students, and no doubt with much greater poetic effect. It takes some practice, but not all that much, and soon a class will be rhyming one-, two-, three-, and even four-syllable words and phrases almost obsessively. My advice is to hold brainstorming sessions (see Chapter 1, on skin poetry) and competitions, and to devote a writing or bulletin board to recording and celebrating the most clever rhymes that students come up with, as an aid to writing.

Beyond the use of sound and rhythm through rhyming, hip-hop and spoken word depend on three poetic elements of meaning for their punch: wordplay, or the use of double entendre; metaphor (and simile); and careful selection of uncommon words and often the possession of a multisyllabic vocabulary.

Wordplay is, simply, playing around with the multiple meanings and uses of words. Most words in the English language, and in particular the most common ones, frequently have many different meanings, some of which may even conflict with one another, depending on the context of their use. The trick to using wordplay in hip-hop and spoken word is first to identify the multiple meanings of a key word in a line and then see how a different meaning or use of a word might enhance or add some irony to a rapper's lyrics. For example, in the phrase "hip-hop game" in the line of poetry above, "But I'm tellin' ya, it's all a part of my hip-hop game," the "game" could be not a contest, but a wild animal to be hunted, like a rabbit ("hip-hop"; get it?). In a "battle" between two rappers, this might lead my opponent to counter:

> Your rhymes are game, all right, like the kind that hip-hops
> Keep on rhyming like that, and you'll be stew in a pot.

Again, this sort of wordplay is easier than it initially seems. It simply takes a willingness to look beyond the first, or intended meaning of a word within a line and then play around with that line or extend an idea to a second line, to see how meaning might be reversed or added to. Escher (2006) urges beginning rappers to make lists and keep notebooks of multiple meanings that come to mind for common words, as a way of developing *the habit* of "going random" (see Chapter 2)—that is, of finding new ways to make language work *for* speakers rather than *on* them.

A second and closely related element that is frequently used in hip-hop and spoken word is the extended metaphor or simile. In the two lines above, for example, the word "game" is played on, but the line also contains a metaphor (or simile) that extends the twist, "like the kind that hip-hops." Popular culture and political images are especially prevalent sources of metaphor in hip-hop and spoken word, as in this example:

> Just like Obama,
> I'm a man without drama.

Or this one, in reference to the movie series *Transformers*:

> In a twist, rhymes transform her
> Like Optimus Prime, she gives no corner.

Or this one (supply your own meaning here):

> Your shake-n-bake is my hamburger helper.

The last element of hip-hop and spoken word that is not only critical to writing in the genre but to literate development of all sorts is the acquisition and use of relatively uncommon, and again often multisyllabic, vocabulary words. While this is not true of all commercial rappers, many artists, particularly within the traditions of slam and spoken word, rely heavily on the use of big, juicy, multisyllabic words, particularly when it comes to the creation of a jaw-dropping, show-stopping multie. For teachers, the writing of hip-hop and spoken word is also obviously a great opportunity to do some vocabulary development in a highly engaging way.

The best way to introduce big, juicy vocabulary words into the writing of hip-hop or spoken word poetry is to begin with the rough drafts of students' work and, as a revision exercise, have students identify key words in their raps that are ordinary and then use a combination of reference works as sources of new, more elaborate vocabulary. For example, a student might write a line with the expression "a (bad) attitude." A consultation with an online thesaurus, like Thesaurus.com, yields dozens of entries, including *disposition, proclivity,* and *posture,* but the one that catches his eye is *predilection.* Now, of course, a synonym is not a synonym is not a synonym, so to be sure that "predilection" refers to the sort of (bad) attitude that he means, he consults Dictionary.com or one of many other online dictionaries, and learns that a predilection is a preference or a predisposition, but usually toward something, not away from it. This is close; but how will he work the "bad" part into the phrase? And it would be cool if it would rhyme . . . predilection, collection, direction . . . Ah! *Correction!* A bit more play with the phrase and he has it: A (bad) attitude is now "a predilection in need of correction."

In another example, a student has the phrase "trial by fire" in one of her lines and decides it needs a boost. Again, she searches

Thesaurus.com, this time for two words, "trial" and "fire," and quickly comes up with two words that rhyme: "adjudication" and "conflagration." A bit of checking with the dictionary and some play with the phrase and a trial by fire becomes an "adjudication by conflagration." In a last example, a student wants to let her audience know that she's "straight up"—that is, she's giving her honest opinion about an issue. She searches "straight up" in her online thesaurus, but only finds meanings related to direction and cooking, not to honesty. She searches "tell the truth" and finds only simple words, but also an antonym: "lie." On a hunch, she searches "lie," and one word catches her attention: "prevaricate." But what rhymes with that? And, it's the opposite of what she means. This time, the student is stumped. But her teacher has an idea, and begins to spin words beginning with *p* and ending in *ate*: procreate, placate, prostrate, *prognosticate*. Prognosticate? She checks the dictionary and finds that it means to predict or foretell the future. But it also means to see through events, or to have insight, or *to see the true situation.* She suggests this word to the student, and they play around with the phrasing, coming up eventually with "I prognosticate, not prevaricate"—a phrase that slightly turns the original sentiment without misdirecting its meaning.

The search for vocabulary that will transform common words and phrases into jaw droppers and show stoppers is not a completely mechanical process of looking up words in a thesaurus, checking their meaning with a dictionary, and then searching for words that rhyme. Oftentimes students do not have sufficient flexibility in their language skills to try different key words or to think to search an opposite. And it is also the case that the available search engines are not always elaborate enough to narrow possibilities or expand them as needed. These are points where teachers, practice, and patience are needed, and where the use of word walls—collections of vocabulary words developed by students and teachers that are displayed on bulletin boards—and other practices for developing vocabulary are indispensable. (For more on word walls, see theteacherscorner.net and click "lesson plans," then "writing.") Yet in spite of these difficulties, it is very much worth taking the time and making the effort as students revise and rehearse their raps for performance to pick out a phrase here and there in each and work with them to find big, juicy vocabulary words that will impress and delight *and empower* themselves and their audience.

SPOKEN WORD IN THE CLASSROOM

Before our field tests for this book I had never taught hip-hop or spoken word poetry in a secondary school classroom before. However, two teachers in the project, Ms. Hendrick and Ms. Lewis, were eager to have us work with their students, several of whom were amateur rappers with stage names and a growing repertoire of raps.

We planned for these challenges by providing examples of the types of hip-hop or spoken word poetry that we were hoping students would model. We turned to four examples on YouTube. Using Zamzar.com, we downloaded and converted "The Day Hip-Hop Died" from YouTube.com, the opening piece to the 2006 Urban Word NYC Teen Poetry Slam, as our opening example. We also converted a short video by an anonymous rapper giving advice about "how to write a good rap song" from YouTube, a performance describing the power of writing hip-hop (search: The Hip Hop Project), and finally, a very creative example of a "cypher," in which a group of poets sit in a circle and improvise off one another's lyrics (search: Cypher Game).

In showing these short videos at the outset of the assignment, we hoped to shift the students' perspectives about hip-hop away from the violence and misogynistic themes of some commercial artists and toward the aesthetics and sensibilities of the spoken word/youth poetry slam tradition. We also discussed each video briefly, asking students for their evaluation of the performances, and suggested features or ideas that they might incorporate into their writing and performance. In both classrooms, the students were keen to write and several volunteered to "spit," or perform from memory, rhymes they had already written.

Once students had begun to put ideas and words on paper, we introduced and worked to develop their knowledge of the elements of rhyme, metaphor, and allusion that are characteristic of hip-hop and spoken word, such as slant rhyme, multies, wordplay, and the use of big, juicy vocabulary. We introduced these with a PowerPoint presentation and a handout that summarized and provided examples of each, and then circulated among the students, reading their lines aloud and trying to stimulate brainstorming sessions that would generate more complex rhymes and use of language. In a final session, the students presented their poems and we videotaped and played back their performances.

Ms. Hendrick's Classroom

In both classrooms, the students' poems were divided between themes that were intensely personal and expressed deep vulnerability and those that were often more technically proficient but also less personal and more imitative of commercial hip-hop artists. In Ms. Hendrick's classroom, an African-American and a White girl teamed up to share ideas about their families, including problems with brothers:

> Your brother's attitude gets out of hand
> He goes to school just to get banned.

Several of the boys in this class announced that they were rappers at the outset of the assignments, and their poems were imitative of the braggadocio and language of their favorite rappers. Daniel, however, who was a teenage father, chose to write about his son:

> You make me better than better was
> If you can do better do better than ever done
> . . . Within my pores is a bear that's vicious
> But when I look at you, you bring me back to my senses.
> . . . You want to know why I teach you A.B.C.s
> So you can eat pizza in that leanin' tower overseas.
> My feelings and emotions I'll write on this pad
> Because when I was growing up I didn't see my dad.
> And that's why everyday you bring me joy
> And pride to say that's my boy.

Ms. Lewis's Classroom

In Ms. Lewis's class, two girls—Brandi, who was African American, and Teri, who was White—teamed up to write about the response of their peers to their friendship:

Brandi:	I'm Black
Teri:	I'm White
Brandi:	But it don't matter cuz we'll always be tight
Brandi:	We don't care about these racial slurs
Teri:	We don't care about these racial terms

Brandi:	We're not like these parasites and worms.
Together:	We don't follow the words we hear, We follow what's in here.

EXTENDING THE APPROACH: THREE AUTHORS WITH A BEAT

For teachers interested in extending their knowledge of spoken word/hip-hop and its educational implications, I can suggest three outstanding books. *Writing in Rhythm: Spoken Word Poetry in Urban Classrooms* by Maisha T. Fisher (2007) provides a lively account of the Power Writers, a group of high school students in the Bronx. Under the mentoring of their teacher Joe, the students learned to build from "Bronxonics"—the language, the rhythm, and the performative style of the Bronx, where hip-hop originated—voices and a presentational confidence that bridged the acquisition of "standard" English and helped them to develop the ability to be themselves, both at home and in the world at large. In the course of their studies, writing, and performance the students also learned to "catch words"—to seek out and acquire facility in the use of new vocabulary and to read not only their own writing but the writing of others more closely and with a critical eye for sound and sensibility. Fisher's account does not provide a procedural how-to for reproducing Joe's curriculum, but it does offer some very practical lessons for teachers who are interested in "decolonizing" the English language arts by building on the linguistic and aesthetic gifts that students bring with them to the classroom.

A similar but more conventionally "literary" and more broadly curricular approach to working with spoken word/hip-hop in schools is offered by Marc Lamont Hill in *Beats, Rhymes, and Classroom Life: Hip-Hop Pedagogy and the Politics of Identity* (2009). Hill developed a course called Hip-Hop Lit, which he taught in a "Twilight Program"—an after-school program at a Philadelphia high school that was offered in the late afternoon to students "who do not fit comfortably within the day school environment" (p. 15). But whereas the students in Fisher's study focused on developing their own voices through writing and performing original works, Hill's curriculum focused on the close reading and literary analysis of published hip-hop by artists such as Tupac, Jay-Z, and

Grandmaster Flash and the Furious Five. From these and other groups Hill selected poems that reflected a range of themes and literary elements, such as allusion, hyperbole, and allegory. The recognition and analysis of these elements and students' responses to them through journal writing, sharing, and group reading provided the context for discussions that were not only literary but political and ultimately liberatory for the students. Hill also provides a very scholarly, theoretical rationale that connects hip-hop as a form with students' collective cultural memories. The final chapters of the book move "toward," but do not prescribe, ways in which hip-hop culture could and should be integrated into urban school curriculum "to enhance student motivation, transmit subject area knowledge, and develop habits of mind appropriate for learning" (p. 123).

A third resource, *Hip Hop Speaks to Children: A Celebration of Poetry with a Beat*, edited by Nikki Giovanni (2008), offers an extraordinary resource of poems, a CD with recorded readings by noted poets such as Gary Soto, Eloise Greenfield, Nikki Giovanni, and even Langston Hughes, with recorded commentary by Giovanni and others. The book is a contemporary treasury of multicultural poetry suitable for both children and early adolescents. Each poem in this picture book is accompanied by lively, full-color illustrations in various styles, and many of the poems are accompanied by recordings whose tracks on the CD are easily accessed, particularly by using a laptop. Not all of the poems are, strictly speaking, hip-hop; but all are written and meant to be read or recited, as Giovanni notes, with a beat that stretches across the aesthetic and cultural histories of many different Americans, and which connects the traditions of the past with the performers and poets of today. This book is beautiful and should be a treasured resource of every urban, suburban, or rural elementary and middle-school language arts teacher in the United States today.

SPOKEN WORD POETRY IN A HIGH-STAKES WORLD

Among all the approaches described in this book, none is potentially easier to justify across a broader range of areas within state or provincial standards than hip-hop and spoken word poetry. Spoken word's extensive and complex use of metaphor, allusion, and wordplay, the attention it draws to students' awareness of phonetic nuance and rhyme, and its opportunities for vocabulary development, are reflected directly in the standards of nearly every state and province in North America, from California to Colorado to Connecticut, and from British Columbia to New Brunswick. Moreover, with its focus on complex rhyme patterns and clever use of a variety of figures of speech, hip-hop and spoken word create an outstanding bridge from youth popular culture to the poetics of older, more canonical forms of English-language verse. If you teach hip-hop in your classroom, and particularly if you pair lessons in particular hip-hop elements with examples of the same elements from the work of Shakespeare, Chaucer, Keats, or Dickinson, your students will grasp the continuity of English poetics across history and your colleagues and community will have to think twice before they accuse you of selling out or giving up on Our Literary Heritage.

But I also want to note here that simply encouraging students to write and perform hip-hop poems within an English classroom is no guarantee that standards will be "covered," or, far more important, that students' formal knowledge and understanding of the basics of English poetics will necessarily develop. All the students in our project were eager to rap, but they were less eager—or perhaps we were not fully prepared or did not make the time to teach them how—to thoughtfully revise, that is, to select words or phrases or rhymes and rework them into the jaw-dropping, show-stopping, big, juicy vocabulary words, multies, or metaphors that are the hallmark of "the dopest flows" in the genre. In retrospect, we wish that we had had more time to develop the multiple elements that comprise the basics of hip-hop, perhaps through mini-lessons over a period of weeks rather than only 2 or 3 days, and to connect what the students were learning to do with similar practices of poets from the past.

KEEP IN MIND

- Hip-hop and spoken word poetry are very complex art forms whose elements cannot be taught well in just a few days.
- Be prepared. Be sure to have plenty of examples of slant rhyme, multies, different rhyme schemes,

metaphors, wordplay, and big, juicy vocabulary words available, both in isolation and within the lyrics of hip-hop artists (for lyrics, see www.ohhla.com/all. html). Finding video examples of spoken word through YouTube or other Internet providers is also extremely helpful, particularly in the beginning stages of the writing process.

- Take plenty of time for revision and for reintroducing different elements through short reviews or mini-lessons.
- It is important to push students to move beyond their first drafts and experiment with rhymes and figures of speech, but as in the case of blues poetry (see Chapter 3), there is no need to be overly formulaic or to set quotas for "three multies" or "two examples of wordplay" in students' final drafts. Instead, you'll keep students' enthusiasm and engagement high if you work with them to brainstorm ideas for different elements as the need arises within the revision process. Organizing students into small groups rather than giving them individual assignments is also helpful the first or second time students write hip-hop.

CHAPTER 5

Digital Performance

Remixing the Masters Multimodally

Multimodality is the crafted integration of two or more ways, or modes, of communication, so that their combined meaning as a whole is greater than either mode separately or their simple combination. A teacher who coordinates an explanation with a simple sketch or diagram on a whiteboard, an opera diva who sings an aria dressed in a lavish costume as she gestures toward her lover, and a television producer who mixes maps, motion pictures, and voice-over narration in a newscast are all communicating their messages multimodally. In each of these examples, the individual modes communicate a message on their own, but in combination their message is multiplied and becomes far more engaging, far more comprehensible, and far more interpretable for their audience.

Although the term is rather recent, the concept is surely as old as human culture. The pictographic remains on cave walls in France and the U.S. Southwest were visual aids used by shamans to explain their spirit journeys, and the architecture of ancient Mesoamerican monuments, in coordination with their positioning in relation to other landmarks and to the sun, conveyed powerful messages about people's relationship to the universe. With the invention of writing, the use of print script with images on Egyptian, Mayan, Sumerian, and Chinese monuments made the communication of complex narratives and systems of thought transmittable across vast expanses of time and space. Illustrated medieval manuscripts, the Gutenberg Bible, children's books, modern newspapers, billboards, and posters are also examples of multimodal texts.

Digital literacy at the beginning of the 21st century is therefore not new because of its multimodality, but like the invention of movable print in 15th-century Europe, its development does signal an enormous step forward in ordinary people's ability to participate in discussions about the big issues and ideas that shape their communities, their nations, and the world, for two reasons. The first is that with the advent of affordable, ubiquitous computer technologies, digital cameras, and virtual space—still free!—provided through services such as YouTube, Google, Blogger, and Twitter, nearly every moderately well-educated and literate individual in every industrialized and the majority of industrializing countries in the world has the opportunity to become her or his own publisher. Anyone who can find access to a computer and the Internet can make a video and post it on YouTube or start their own blog or participate in any of a million chat rooms and special interest group sites online. I don't mean to overstate an individual's probable audience (at least initially) or the immediate impact of her message on the course of human events, but looking at the impact that YouTube postings have had on elections or the impact of Twitter on events in Iran, that potential should not be dismissed, either.

The second reason is the range of modes that digital communication adds to ordinary people's communicative tool kit. In predigital times, a student could build a model or make a poster and support these with a live speech, but preserving the entire presentation and making it available to a wide audience would have been prohibitively expensive in most cases. The ability of digital technologies to fuse audio and video recordings along with print text, photographs, diagrams, and moving images in one document, and to do so using software that provides infinite revision and a professional, high-quality appearance dramatically changes what it means to write or compose a "text." And the ability to upload that document to a central archive, or server, and then provide access to as few or as many people as one wants or needs, expands the capacity of students and teachers to communicate with others across time and space in ways that have barely been imagined yet, much less explored.

In short, and high-stakes accountability and standards-based curriculum aside, this is the most exciting time to be a literacy educator in the past 500 years. This is true not only because the nature of texts and how they are composed and comprehended is literally shifting under teachers' and students' eyes and ears, but because there is no better way to explore the potential of the new digital tools than by applying them to a "remixing" of classic texts—especially short, tightly constructed ones like poems—in ways that open them to new avenues of interpretation by readers and/or writers.

Although in this chapter I will explore a number of different technological approaches to "remixing" the masters, as the main example I have chosen an approach that was first developed by Mary McVee and her colleagues at the University at Buffalo in New York. For several years, McVee and her colleagues have assigned preservice teachers a multimodal remixing of a poem using PowerPoint that combines a personal response to a short lyric poem with a "performance" of the poem that uses video, sound, and advanced animation features of the software. In an article based on this teaching that I was proud to edit for *Research in the Teaching of English*, "Using Digital Media to Interpret Poetry: Spiderman Meets Walt Whitman" (McVee, Bailey, & Shanahan, 2008), McVee and her colleagues provide an analysis of one student's PowerPoint interpretation of "A Noiseless Patient Spider" by Walt Whitman. This PowerPoint and two others can be viewed online at multimodalpoetry.org. The link to this site and all sites in this chapter is available at letspoemresources.ning.com.

The student Laura's work is a truly remarkable example of how digital technology can add meaning and personal depth to the work of a canonical poet. Laura was a graduate student and a mother, and her reading of Whitman opens with a short video, presumably of her daughter, sitting on a swing and singing "The Itsy-Bitsy Spider." In the next slide, she presents a short biographical commentary on the life of Whitman, and this is followed by a presentation of the poem itself, which includes the selection of different fonts for particular words and phrases that fade in and move on the screen as cues to how she intends them to be read, accompanied by a recording of a piano solo. When the presentation comes to the line "It launched forth filament," the word "filament" is repeated three times, each time moving in a curve from the lower right to the upper right corner of the screen. The next slide uses a thin moving line (a "filament") to illustrate two phrases.

But then the reading becomes very interesting, even provocative. In the next slide, the line "And you, O my Soul, where you stand" is accompanied by a photo of the dual personas of Spiderman and Peter Parker from the movie series. The Spiderman "reading" of the poem continues in the next slides, as words and phrases of the poem are presented in *iconic* representations of their meanings. For example, the word "surrounded" in the poem is presented in a curved font that forms a circle around the words that follow, "In measureless oceans of space." In another slide, the word "bridge" in the line "Till the bridge you will need be form'd" dissolves into a photo of the finger of Adam touching the finger of God on the ceiling of the Sistene Chapel—a photo that links, in turn, two photographs of bridges. In the final slides, Laura returns to the theme of family that began the presentation, showing (presumably) photos from her wedding and other images of her current identity.

McVee described the power of the digital poetry project in this way:

> In looking across student reflections, we found that students who had negative feelings about poetry repeatedly wrote about shifting their gaze away from their emotions about poetry toward communicating meaning. As students began to think about how a poem could be represented visually, aurally, or through on-screen movement, they focused on how to communicate the meanings that they wanted others to experience. This moved them away from fears that they would not produce a "correct" interpretation. Instead, they were intent on exploring various modalities to communicate meanings they were discovering. Although at times the technology glitches or learning curve frustrated participants, they learned to see the computer and software programs not as technical skills they must learn for the sake of "learning technology" but as mediators that helped them create signs used for communicative purposes. (p. 132)

TEACHING ADVANCED POWERPOINT

The first time I saw Laura's PowerPoint at a conference presentation by Mary McVee, I was bowled over. This living, moving, beautiful presentation was made with PowerPoint?! There is a line of argument in educational theory and research that PowerPoint's bulleted formatting, emphasis on short phrases, and canned templates are producing The End of Thoughtful Discourse in modern communication. However, once the preformatted slides and templates of the program are ignored in favor of a blank slide format and handmade backgrounds, and the animation, transition, and visual and audio insertion features of the program are explored, PowerPoint becomes a remarkably flexible, relatively intuitive, and ubiquitous, utterly available tool for producing highly original multimodal texts.

But the quote from Mary McVee above also points to some serious concerns with PowerPoint, namely its "technical glitches" in the form of inserted video and audio clips that won't play on some computers, incompatibility between versions (e.g., presentations made with the 2007 version are distorted when played on the 2003 program), storage of in-progress drafts, and the technical complexity of some animation, timing, and sequencing features. All of these issues are either avoidable or resolvable, but doing so takes a good deal of planning, organization, consistency, and expertise that ought not to be obtained on the fly. Based on my own experiences teaching the advanced animation features of PowerPoint, here is my primer for how to avoid the most serious problems with the program.

First, I would decide which version of the program to use with my class and stick to it. By now, the 2003 version of PowerPoint (PPT) is rapidly disappearing, but it may still be the case that some computers in your school are running it. Be sure that only one version is being used, because the menus of the 2003 and 2007 versions are quite different and switching back and forth between them is very confusing. Moreover, a PPT begun on a 2003 version will transfer poorly to the 2007 version, and vice versa.

Second, for any software program you choose to introduce it is critical that you master the program first before trying to teach it to students. It is probably the case that you have used PPT before for presentations, but learning how to animate text and other images, insert video and audio successfully, and adjust sequencing and transitions within and between slides takes skill and effort. My advice is to try to make a multimodal PPT presentation yourself before you assign the task to students. You can then use the PPT as a model for demonstrating different techniques. If you get stuck, the Microsoft PowerPoint page at office.microsoft.com (click on "Help and How-to") provides excellent tutorials. Another very teacher-friendly site is "PowerPoint in the Classroom," at actden.com/PP.

When you're ready to plan a class activity, depending on how proficient your students already are with the basics of PPT and what you know of their work habits, you should probably allot 5 to 10 days of in-class work (assuming 50-minute periods) to complete the project. If you're using computers that other students will have access to during this time (as in a lab setting), you'll need to arrange for students to be able to save their work-in-progress in a secure location, such as in individual folders on the school's server. Finally, instead of assigning students to work on individual projects (imagine 25 hands raised all at once, needing your assistance with a glitch), it makes much more sense to organize students into groups of three or four, and perhaps to survey the students first about their level of expertise with PPT so that you can spread the "experts" around in the groups. This will also speed up the work, since some students in a group can be searching for images, video, and audio online while others work on the PPT itself.

Start small. Don't try to multimodally remix "The Rime of the Ancient Mariner" or any longer narrative or lyric poem. A haiku or an Emily Dickinson poem will provide more than enough challenge; even a blues poem or a sonnet may be too long for some groups of students to complete in their first attempt.

Before you begin to teach, be sure you have organized your steps for composing into a careful sequence, such as the one presented in the box shown here. Once students have found (or you have provided) a poem to remix, perhaps after a visit to Poets.org or PoetryFoundation.org they'll need to open PPT and begin to organize the lines of the poem, one line per slide (usually), by typing in the line in a text box on a blank-formatted slide. The students should save their work as a PPT file, and put the file *inside a folder*. This is absolutely critical, because once the students begin to insert video and audio files into their PPTs, they'll need to put those files into the same folder first *before* they insert them. It is important to know that photos, text, and animation instructions are embedded

A Sequence for Composing a Multimodal PowerPoint

1. For this project, go to Poets.org and select a short poem of 6–8 lines that you'd like to animate.
2. Go through the poem and divide it into a number of short lines per PowerPoint slide.
3. Create a folder on your desktop.
4. Open PowerPoint and save your file in the folder on your desktop. Begin to select background colors, designs, etc. You do not need to select a preset design background; you can customize.
5. Now, you can do a couple of things or work back and forth among them: select music, select photos, select a font and colors for the font.
6. Begin to type the lines of the poem on each slide. As you work, imagine how you might make the words move, appear or disappear, and so on, to represent the ideas of the poem. Work on a blank slide (one without any layout). Create text boxes for the different words and phrases that you'd like to animate.
7. Go to "custom animation" on the slide menu and experiment with entrances, exits, and other animations. Also be sure to work on the timing and the order (sequence) of the effects. You can move the order of effects by clicking and dragging them.
8. DON'T WORRY—You can't break PowerPoint and everything can be fixed!
9. Select music, narration (your voice), or other audio. Put these files in the desktop folder *before* you insert them into your PowerPoint.
10. Insert your audio in the slide where you want it to begin. You can control where the audio stops and starts.
11. Select "slide transition." You can time how long each slide lasts on the screen and sync this with the music. If you don't do this you'll need to change each slide manually and the animated effect will be partially lost.
12. Work back and forth through the PowerPoint to make sure all the transitions and timing are correct.
13. Congratulations—you've created a multimodal, animated "remixing" of a poem!

within a PPT file and therefore stay with that file wherever it is moved; but audio and video files *do not embed.* Instead, only the location and directions for the audio or video file are embedded, so that if an audio or video file is not in the folder with the PPT, once the PPT is transferred to another computer or location, the connection to the video or audio file will be lost.

Finally, once the multimodal PPT is completed and will play smoothly on the computer, it is important to "package" or "publish" the file. In the 2003 version, this is accomplished by clicking on the "File" tab and then scrolling down the menu to the "Package for CD" option, and in the 2007 version, by clicking the Office button, scrolling down to "Publish" and then clicking "Package for CD."

There are additional steps you can take to convert your PPT to other formats that may be more durable over time. These are listed on letspoemresources.ning.com.

MULTIMODALITY IN THE CLASSROOM

We field-tested composing multimodal PPTs of poetry with students in Ms. Hendrick's and Ms. Parker's classrooms. Ms. Hendrick's students were a diverse group of 9th graders whose test scores placed them well above the average scores for their school in literacy. Nearly all of the students had used PowerPoint before and two, Tim and Mike, had used PPT to compose "make your own adventure" games. Most of the students in the class, however, had never used the animation or transition features of the program before.

We followed the sequence of steps described in this chapter for the composition process. The students quickly formed themselves into groups on the first day of class, moved to computers in the back of Ms. Hendrick's classroom, and selected poems from multiple online sources. This was a relatively simple process because most of the groups already had particular poems in mind, and others were open to Ms. Hendrick's and my suggestions. The next day we decided we needed a bit more space than Ms. Hendrick's room allowed, and moved to a computer lab. The students were able to log in to their spaces on the school's server, create a folder, and open and save a PPT document. The students created a number of blank slides and typed in the lines of poetry for each that they wanted to animate, saving and resaving as they worked. Then the process slowed as the students began to search for images online, use these as background and photographs, and choose fonts, text sizes, and colors for each line and word of their poems. It was a challenge for us to move from group to group and troubleshoot small problems, but with some effort the students gained confidence ("You can't break the program," I reminded them; and "Don't worry about making a mistake; it can always be fixed.") over the course of the period.

By the 3rd day, when we had moved again to a bank of computers in the school library and the slides began to take shape, quick progress began to be made. Once the basic backgrounds and text features had been selected for each slide, the groups began to divide tasks among members. Some students worked on the animation and transition features of the slides, some searched (on other computers) for additional images, and others, with suggestions from us, browsed music files online for recordings that fit the theme and tone of their poems. Using e-mail accounts, the students sent what they had found to the students composing the PPT, then worked with them to combine and refine each slide and to animate the texts. In some cases students chose preset animation features ("fade in," "blinds," "swivel") for particular words or phrases; in other cases, they created motion paths for words or images and used advanced timing features to make words and images move in unique fashions. Once these features were completed, the students inserted music files and then timed the sequence of animation features and slide transitions in time with the music. Altogether, the projects were completed in six class sessions.

All of the students' projects were vibrant, iconic renderings of well-known poems, but two in particular stand out. Four African-American students—Alicia, Maya, Roberta, and Chaz—chose the poem "We Real Cool," by Gwendolyn Brooks. This is a very short poem, and the students complemented its short, staccato lines with images that shifted color from slide to slide and which were very bright and vibrant. They selected a saxophone jazz tune that was suggested by Ms. Hendrick as their sound track; it represented the poem's final lines, "We jazz June/We die soon." They also included a bright red background and a photograph of a saxophone, above which each letter appeared individually, as though it were being typed.

Another group of two students, Tim and Mike, selected a passage from a translation of "The Iliad." These students had advanced skills using PowerPoint, and made strong use of them. One student browsed online for tunes and originally responded to my suggestion that they use something from "Carmina Burana" by Carl Orff. In the end, however, they selected "The Final Countdown" by the band Europe, and timed the transitions of their slides to passages in the music. As befitted the war theme of the passage, the transitions from slide to slide were sudden spirals out of one slide and into another, and they used dramatic entrance and exit effects for the text.

The students in Ms. Parker's class were younger and at a different point in their development, both as users of computer technology and with regard to their literate development. In a variation on the assignment, they used PowerPoint to animate the texts of the skin poems (see Chapter 2) that they had written. Although much simpler, these compositions were multimodal in their use of images collected from the Internet and selection of animation effects for text that complemented the ideas they were expressing.

EXTENDING THE APPROACH: OTHER MULTIMODAL PROGRAMS AND FORMATS

Of course, neither PowerPoint nor Microsoft has a monopoly on production options for digital multimodal texts. My emphasis on it in this chapter has to do with its wide availability, its animation features, and the fact that nearly all teachers and students have some familiarity with the program. Other multimodal programs that I would suggest composing with are the multiple video editing programs available on the market, including iMovie and Windows Movie Maker, which are included in the service packages of Apple computers and PCs that run Windows operating systems and Adobe Premiere (for information on using Apple equivalents of Windows applications, go to: letspoemresources.ning.com. Apple.com is also an excellent online resource). All of these editing programs make it possible for a multimodal composer to upload video clips, photographs, and audio in various formats (music files, voice narration, and other sound clips), and to combine these with a poem whose lines are presented as title overlays within the video.

Remixing a poem multimodally using a video editing program is in many ways simpler than taking the PowerPoint route, but it also has two distinct disadvantages. The first is that the computer on which a teacher or student begins to compose is the computer and program they must continue to work on until the project is complete. Unlike a PowerPoint presentation, which is a *document* that can be transferred from one computer to another as long as both computers have the same version of PowerPoint, a video-editing program simply assembles the various clips, photos, and other features of a video project and holds them within the program until the composer and/or editor decides the project is complete and then clicks a button that *compresses* the different elements into a single, final video file (either .mov, .wmv, or .avi, usually). A word of caution, then, is that once you decide that your video is done, you should not forget to click the button on the program to "produce" or "compress" or otherwise turn the project into a finalized video file. Otherwise the project file will either not open at all, or only open with some of your files (usually with titles, but no photos, videos, or audio clips) when played on another computer.

The second disadvantage is that video-editing programs almost never include animation features that would enable you to make words appear and disappear or move around on a screen the way text and other images can be animated using PowerPoint. This means that Laura's multimodal remixing of "A Noiseless Patient Spider" using Movie Maker or iMovie would have lacked the animated filaments or other motion elements that made the presentation of the text of the poem so dynamic and *iconic*, so that the words as images were made to resemble their meanings. There are animation programs on the market, such as Adobe Flash, that would enable animation of a text in ways that matched or exceeded the capabilities of PowerPoint, but these remain expensive, rare, or nonexistent in most schools, and are even more complicated to use than PowerPoint.

An entirely different multimodal approach to interpreting poetry that does make excellent use of video-editing programs is a project that is based on the Favorite Poem Project (favoritepoem. org). This project was initiated by U.S. Poet Laureate Robert Pinsky in 1997 and continues today. It features short (3- to 5-minute) videos of people from all walks of life reading their favorite poem and explaining its significance to them and their lives. The videos are available online at the Favorite Poem website, and feature a wide variety of poems. In my teaching of preservice teacher education courses, I've had students produce "International Favorite Poem" videos, in which small groups of students ask a foreign student at my university to read their favorite poem in their native language (for example, Chinese, Hindi, Spanish, or Greek) and then in translation. The project not only expands English majors' knowledge of poetry outside the Anglophone tradition; it also teaches them the basics of editing video.

The "favorite poem" video idea can have many variations, of course, in terms of the exact topic and group of students/readers with whom a teacher is working. I would strongly suggest again that this be a small group project, that a teacher should have had some experience with video editing beforehand, and that, like the PowerPoint project, at least 5–10 class periods (or more) be allotted to production. In terms of equipment, the project would require at minimum a webcam or video camera, either digital or using digital videotape, a tripod, and a computer with either iMovie, Movie-Maker, or another video editing program installed. The computer should also have a significant amount of memory available (video takes up a lot of space) and advanced graphics processing capability. More detailed information on how to use video editing software is beyond the scope of this chapter. However, there are many excellent online video tutorials available, such as at the Windows.com site (click on "Help and How-to"), "Tips for Using Movie Maker" at ReadWriteThink.org, and the tutorial site at Apple.com (search for "iMovie").

MULTIMODALITY IN A HIGH-STAKES WORLD

Although the emphasis on "basics" of most states' and provinces' learning standards would seem to conflict with the "complex" and "advanced" quality of multimodal composing processes, using PowerPoint, iMovie, or other software to "remix" or otherwise creatively interpret great poetry is not difficult to justify, either as an application of technology or as an exercise in reading or literary response. In New York, for instance, Grades 9–12 Standard 2 (writing for literary response and expression), Standard 3 (writing for critical analysis and evaluation), and Standard 4 (writing for social interaction) all require that students "[u]se computer technology to create, manipulate, and edit text"). New York State Standard 2 also requires students to "[u]se resources such as personal experience, knowledge from other content areas, and independent reading to create imaginative, interpretive, and responsive texts."

Similarly, Standard 1.8 (Writing) of the California English Language Arts Content Standards for Grades 9–10 requires students to "[d]esign and publish documents by using advanced publishing software and graphic programs." Standard 3.8 (Reading) requires students to "[i]nterpret and evaluate the impact of ambiguities, subtleties, contradictions, ironies, and incongruities in a text." In Ontario, Grades 9–10 Academic Media Studies Expectation 3.4 states that students should "produce media texts for several different purposes and audiences, using appropriate forms, conventions, and techniques." Similarly, Grade 8 Writing Expectation 3.7 states that students will "use a wide range of appropriate elements of effective presentation in the finished product, including print, script, different fonts, graphics, and layout" and Media Studies Expectation 3.2 states that students will "identify an appropriate form to suit the purpose and audience for a media text they plan to create."

However, a reading of the standards across multiple states and provinces also implies, and I would strongly agree, that students learn the most not from simply producing a multimodal composition, but before, during, and especially *after* they have presented their PowerPoint or video to an audience and/or to a teacher, who asks them thoughtful, critical questions about their reasons for selecting particular fonts, images, and animation/transition techniques to express particular ideas and feelings in their poems. For example, Ontario Media Studies Expectation 4.1 for grade 8 states that students will "identify what strategies they found most helpful in making sense of and creating media texts, and explain how these and other strategies *can help them improve as media viewers/listeners/ producers* (italics added)." New York Standard 2 (literary response and expression) for speaking states that students will "[u]se media to support presentation of original and interpretive texts" and "[a]sk and respond to questions and follow-up questions to clarify interpretation." Similarly, California Content Standard 2.2 for Speaking (Grades 9–10) states that in delivering responses to literature, students will "[c]onnect (their) own responses to the writer's techniques and to specific textual references," "[d]raw supported inferences about the effects of a literary work on its audience," and "[s]upport judgments through references to the text, other works, other authors, or personal knowledge."

In other words, as cool as multimodal composing is, its greatest educational impact comes not from learning how to use the software, from the outlet for self-expression that it provides, or from its capacity to impress or move an audience, but from the opportunity it provides for the development of metacognitive understanding of how contemporary media moves us as individuals and as a society. A teacher cannot assume that simply because students learn *how* to do something, they will necessarily also learn *why* they're doing it, or how their experience of what they've learned might be extended to a critical reading of related genres and their impact, like television ads, movie trailers, or video games. When students become experts themselves in how to "make an impression" using multimodal texts *and are invited to talk about* why they made particular decisions and the impact of those decisions on their audience, a door is opened for a critique of the ways that advertisers and other media producers use the same tools to make an impression on them.

KEEP IN MIND

Given the technical complexity of multimodal software like PowerPoint and iMovie and the potential for glitches and multiple problems whenever instructional technology is used for the first time, it might be reasonable to ask whether composing multimodal remixes of poems is worth the time and the effort. Based on my experiences with preservice teachers and interactions with students and teachers in two classrooms so far, I believe the answer to that question is still an emphatic *yes!* The confidence students develop from the process, the impression their work makes on themselves and others, and the potential critical awareness of how multimedia create impressions on readers and viewers far outweighs the temporary frustration of the learning curve that is an almost unavoidable part of the process. Remember also that most of the frustration and many glitches can be avoided if a few simple practices are followed:

- Be sure as a teacher that you have had the experience of composing first so that you will easily know how to avoid or solve technical problems in your classroom.
- Organize the class into small groups rather than individual assignments.
- Stick to one version of PowerPoint or one video-editing software program for all groups.
- The first time, work with short poems of no more than 6–8 lines.
- Make a folder, put the PPT document in that folder, and add all video and audio files to the folder before inserting them in the PPT document.
- Have a clear sequence of procedural steps before you begin composing and make sure the students follow that sequence.
- Be sure to "package" your PPT or "compress" your video when it's complete, and if possible convert the PPT into a more stable file format, like .swf or a video format such as .wmv, .avi, or .mov, that will also make it possible to share on a website.
- Be sure to have students explain their reasoning behind decisions about animation, image selection, color, audio, and other elements of their work, with emphasis on how these decisions affect the interpretation of the poem and its effect on an audience.

CHAPTER 6

Global Voices Online

Internationalizing and Diversifying Your Curriculum

As a middle and high school English teacher in pre-Internet days, one of the greatest challenges I faced in teaching poetry was gaining quick and easy access to poems that were relevant to the lives and backgrounds of the students I was teaching, beyond standard anthologies of African-American and Latina/o poetry. In the new millennium, this trend seems to persist. The secondary English education majors I work with at the University of Illinois at Urbana-Champaign seem to know a great deal about the British Romantics and American poets of the early 20th century and the Harlem Renaissance, but almost nothing of contemporary poets, poets from postcolonial countries, or poets whose work is translated from their native languages into English. The extraordinary cultural diversity of North American classrooms today means that the range of texts read and responded to within English language arts classrooms needs to expand dramatically in the coming years.

The good news is that the Internet offers an extraordinary opportunity for teachers to expand the repertoire of poetic texts available to them and their students in ways that did not exist and that I never dreamed of as a classroom teacher. Within a North American context, there are several major portals available that offer a wide range of poetry from Anglophone and, in translation, major foreign-language poets. In addition, many universities, individual departments and professors, and institutes overseas provide websites on the poetry and literature of a vast range of national, cultural, and linguistic peoples.

This last chapter provides an introduction to these resources and poetic traditions. It begins with a brief review of the major portals online, some of which have been featured in earlier chapters, and continues to introduce poetry resources for all of the inhabited continents and many of the island regions of the world. These resources have been developed independently of one another across varied nations and within multiple contexts. The variety of both commercial and noncommercial sites available is astonishing, and exceeds what I am able to present here; these sites are among the best. My advice for reading the chapter is to browse with a computer at your side, stopping to check particular web addresses as you go, and perhaps adding those that meet your and your students' particular interests to your browser's favorites list. All of the links in this chapter are also available on the website that accompanies this book, letspoemresources.ning.com.

GLOBAL POETRY PORTALS

The two most extensive noncommercial sources of poems and information about poets and poetic forms are sites that have been featured in previous chapters, Poets.org and PoetryFoundation. org. Poets.org is the website of the Academy of American Poets and so, in keeping with that organization's focus, it mainly features the works of American (U.S.) poets, although many famous poets writing in other languages, both contemporary (Pablo Neruda) and classical (Dante Alighieri), are also featured. The site's search engine is also designed to make the retrieval of information and poems by poet, title, or first line efficient, but not by geographic region or cultural group. Nevertheless, as a source of information and poems by Latina/o, African-American, Asian-American, and other cultural groups, such as U.S. poets with Middle Eastern and Caribbean heritage, this site is a good place to start. The site is also a great source of information about published anthologies of poetry from around the world.

The Poetry Foundation is the publisher of *Poetry* magazine, "the oldest monthly devoted to verse in the English-speaking world," according to information on its website. The site, like the magazine, is a nonprofit organization that staunchly defends its independence from any particular group, movement, or institution, and its organization and breadth and depth reflect this commitment (although you won't find much, if any, hip-hop here). Its search engine, or "Poetry Tool," is a marvel. Users can search by poem, poet, audiovisuals, articles, or children's poetry, and within each of these categories, among dozens of other subcategories, including, under "Poets," subcategories of schools/periods and geographic region, including the major U.S. regions and every region of the world. The site also contains thousands of short videos, articles about poets and poetry movements, and links to dozens of literary blogs and related poetry websites. For teachers interested in getting an introduction to the most notable poets and poems of any region of the world, Poetryfoundation.org is a great place to start.

Three other noncommercial sites within the United States also deserve exploration. First, the Public Broadcasting Service (PBS) offers a website for its "Poetry Series" feature of the NewsHour at pbs.org/newshour. Most of the poets featured on this site are contemporary and from the United States, but a significant number of the poets are people of color, and there are also a number of poets from the Middle East and other Islamic nations featured. Nearly all of the poets are featured with video readings of their poems, video interviews, and other segments, including full texts of their poems. A second resource is sponsored by the National Endowment for the Humanities (NEH), at Edsitement.neh.gov. In April 2005, NEH featured a "Forms of Poetry" celebration as part of National

Poetry Month. This site features lesson plans for teaching multiple international poetic forms, from the Arabic ghazal to the Japanese tanka and haiku to more traditional English-language forms like the sonnet.

Third, the University of Illinois at Urbana-Champaign (UIUC) manages a "Modern American Poetry" site (www.english.illinois.edu/maps) that supports the *Anthology of American Poetry* (Nelson, 2000), which is edited by a faculty member at UIUC. At last count, the site featured not poetry but essays, criticism, and links for 161 modern American poets, including many poets of color such as Jimmy Santiago Baca, Amiri Baraka, Lucille Clifton, N. Scott Momaday, and Sherman Alexie. "Modernity" on this site stretches well into the last half of the 19th century. Despite a number of links that do not work, the site operates as an excellent resource for teachers and students who are interested in studying nearly all of the major U.S. poets since the Civil War.

For a truly international selection of poems and poets, begin with Poetry International Web (international.poetryinternationalweb.org), a website based in Rotterdam, the Netherlands, that is funded by a number of national institutions of the Netherlands, the European Union, and elsewhere. This site is organized by poets of individual nations around the world rather than regions or languages, and although all nations are not represented on the site, the sample is quite broad and representative, from most EU nations to Morocco, Angola, China, Japan, Argentina, and the United States. Click on the button for a particular nation, and a list of its major poets appears. Click on the name of a poet, and a brief biography with a short selection of poems by that poet (as few as one or as many as six or seven) appears, both in the poet's native language and in English translation. The site also features many video and audio recordings by noted poets.

A second site that offers a wide array of international poetry in translation is the Open Directory Project (dmoz.org; click on "Arts," then "Literature," then "Poetry"). This site does not directly feature information about poets or poems; instead, it features a wide range of links found online about particular poets, organized by region and nation. Click on "Africa," for instance, and links for 11 major African poets, from Leopold Senghor to David Diop, are offered. The link for "Latin American" poetry is even more extensive, and features multiple links for nine major Latin American poets as well as 11 links to independent websites devoted to the poetry of individual poets and nations. Very often the poems are presented in their original language and in translation, and if there are multiple translations of the same poem offered online, these are listed as well. This is an extraordinary resource for anyone interested in finding foreign-language poetry translated into English.

A third international site worth exploring is PoetSeers.org, a website that was founded as a "collection of spiritual and illumining poetry by poets from around the world, including many different spiritual traditions." The site is organized by theme and by spiritual tradition, although it is possible to search by individual poet and geographic regions as well. The site is edited by two individuals, Abichal Watkins and Tejvan Pettinger. Its selection of poems, poets, and themes is quite extensive, and the site is very well organized.

Two very extensive commercial poetry portals also deserve mention. These sites feature extensive advertising and a good many pop-ups, but if you can get around them, they are also extraordinary sources of international and U.S. poetry. FamousPoetsandPoems.com is a good source of information and poetry by the most popular U.S. and British poets past and present, including many children's poets. Full texts of the most famous poems of these poets (e.g., "Howl," by Alan Ginsberg) are available, but beware of the extensive pop-ups and ads that are featured on every page of the site.

The Poem Hunter (poemhunter.com) features the poetry of literally *thousands* of poets, including both well-known and recognized poets and amateurs who submit their poetry for publication on the site. The site also includes biographies of published poets and an extensive list of categories by topic, such as "love," "war," "summer," and so on. All of the poems on the site are in English and few poets who do not write in English are featured; but the list of English-language poets is exhaustive.

AFRICAN-AMERICAN POETRY

Information and poems written by African-American poets are available on many websites, including nearly all of the sites on the general portals listed in the previous section. For a portal devoted exclusively to African-American poets, try AfroPoets.net—the website of Famous Black Writers, which provides excellent biographical and background information on at least 38 noted African-American poets as well as a selection of five to six poems written by each.

However, the greater trend among contemporary poets—not only of African-American but also Latina/o and those of Native American descent—is the development of personal websites by the individual poets devoted to their work and/or the work of others they would like to promote. For a very interesting and provocative site, go to Ishmael Reed's *Konch Magazine* site (ishmaelreedpub.com), which is maintained by Reed as an online literary magazine that features "those voices that are ignored by the American media." Other websites maintained by noted poets include Rita Dove's home page at the University of Virginia (virginia.edu; search for "Rita Dove") and the official sites of Maya Angelou (mayaangelou.com), Nikki Giovanni (nikki-giovanni.com), Amiri Baraka (amiri-baraka.com), and Elizabeth Alexander (elizabethalexander.net), whose poem "Praise Song for the Day" was written and delivered for the inauguration of President Barak Obama. All of these sites feature biographical information and recordings and books for sale, and some feature recent or major poems.

LATINA/O POETRY

Comprehensive collections of poetry or websites devoted exclusively to the poetry of Latina/os, which includes the work of individuals of Mexican, Puerto Rican, Central American, and Dominican heritage among other Latin countries and cultures, remain elusive. An interesting site that focuses on Latina/o poetry criticism is the online journal *Latino Poetry Review* (latinostudies.nd.edu) and its blogsite, Letras Latinas Blog (latinopoetryreview.blogspot.com). These sites provide some very interesting background information on poets and trends in the field of Latina/o poetry, but the information may be beyond the interest of secondary students.

Again, for in-depth information about individual contemporary Latina/o poets, the best sources may be the websites maintained by the individuals themselves. Jimmy Santiago Baca maintains a very reader-friendly site at jimmysantiagobaca.com, which features a bio and some poems from his published books.

Gary Soto's website (garysoto.com) is very kid-friendly and offers an unpublished short story on its "What's Up?" page. Sandra Cisnernos's site (sandracisneros.com) is very well-developed, and includes reviews, interviews, and even study guides for several of her best-known books, along with many pictures of her life at home and as a public figure.

LATIN AMERICA AND THE CARIBBEAN

English-language sites devoted to the poetry of Latin America and the Caribbean, much of which is not in English but in French, Spanish, and Portuguese, are even harder to find than sites focusing exclusively on the poetry of African-American and Latina/o poets. However, several of the general poetry portals described above, especially the Latin American page of the Open Directory Project (dmoz.org; click on "Arts," then "Literature," then "Latin American") and the Latin American Poets page of Poetseers.org offer an introduction to these poets and their work in English. A third site, Poetry International Web, offers an extensive collection of bios and poems by Colombian poets (colombia.poetryinternationalweb.org), but very little from other Latin American countries.

For Caribbean poets, the best source of information currently available may be Geoffrey Philp's Blogspot (geoffreyphilp.blogspot.com). Philp is a Jamaican author of short stories and poetry, and his blog contains multiple links and blogs about the current literary scene in the Caribbean and South Florida. Much of Philp's work focuses on links between Africa and the Americas. This is an idiosyncratic but very worthwhile source of information for teachers and students.

POSTCOLONIAL MOVES: AFRICA/EUROPE

The modern poetry of Africa has a special resonance to it because so many of Africa's most noted modern poets, particularly in West Africa, figured prominently in both the political and literary independence movements of the late 1950s and 1960s. The French-language poets Sékou Touré of Guinea and Leopold Senghor of Senegal are recognized today not only as major poets in French literature but also as the first leaders of their countries following independence from the French. Senghor, in particular, was both a successful poet and political leader, and remained president of Senegal through its first 20 years as a sovereign state. In Nigeria, the poet Christopher Okigbo, who is considered by many to be modern Africa's greatest poet, served as an officer in the Biafran army and was killed in battle in 1967, while Nigerian Nobel laureate Wole Soyinka lives today in exile after having been accused of treason by the Nigerian government in 1997 for his opposition to military rule.

These poets are also very interesting because of the deliberate use many of them made of European literary traditions and figures in the service of their own countries' independence. Many of the English-language poets and writers of Nigeria took the example of William Butler Yeats's paradoxical use of the language of the oppressor—English in Ireland—in the Irish battle for independence in the early decades of the 20th century as their model for using English in the battle for independence and the establishment of a nationalist identity in their home countries (Saïd, 1993).

Three websites provide an excellent range of resources for teachers and secondary students. The Post Colonial Web (post-colonialweb.org) provides a wide range of pages and information on African writers, including poets, novelists, and essayists. For a selection of poems and short bios of major African poets, go to the African literature page of the Open Directory Project at dmoz.org; click on Arts, Literature, African. A site hosted at the University of Florida provides a very scholarly introduction to African poets writing in French, and includes sample poems from the works of major poets as well as external links and biographical information (uflib.ufl.edu/cm/africana).

Three other more idiosyncratic sites are also worth a visit. Admirers of Christopher Okigbo have created a foundation to preserve the memory of his work, and have developed a website at christopher-okigbo.org. A second site devoted to "modern art images" features dozens of "African love poems" at modernart-images.com/poetry.htm. The third site is a blog, the East African Poet (Eastafricanpoet.blogspot.com), maintained by Junior Kennedy and devoted to the promotion of current poetry in Uganda, Kenya, and Tanzania. This blog also contains links to other blogs maintained by East African writers.

INDIGENOUS VOICES

By "indigenous," I mean the voices of poets in cultural groups that were present in a location before its colonization by a more technologically advanced group, usually European. There are many such groups worldwide, in the highlands of Taiwan and Indonesia, in the Arctic, and across Asia, Africa, and the Americas, but here I am focusing on only two categories—Native Americans and the aborigines of Australia.

Although several anthologies of Australian aboriginal poetry have been published in book form, the range of poems available online seems to be limited to one site (creativespirits.info/aboriginalculture), which lists perhaps ten or so poems. Strangely, these poems appear at first to be anonymous; but a close look to the right of the title of each shows the name of the presumed poet in a very light-colored font.

The range of websites that feature poems written by Native American poets and the offerings on these websites are more extensive, but if you search on your own, beware. There are also many sites on the Internet that contain the poetry of impostors—people who are actually not Native and not associated with any Native group—who, for various reasons, find it romantic or useful (or perhaps lucrative) to self-identify as Native Americans (often Cherokee, in my experience). These sites are usually identifiable by the low quality of the poems featured and especially by the very cheesy, gauzy illustrations of "Indian maidens," wolves, buffalo, and Plains Indian "braves" that are posted on the sites.

In my research, I found three sites that are authentic and that provide a very solid introduction to modern poetry written by Native Americans. The first site, Native Wiki: Storytellers (nativewiki.org), organizes bios, criticism, and selections of poems and other literary forms by regional groups. This site is quite extensive and scholarly, and should be a first stop for teachers and students.

A second site is available at hanksville.org/voyage/indpoem.html. This site is very simple, and features poems by nearly 40 poets, most from southwestern groups in the United States, with some links back to the Native Wiki site. The last site is a single page from Native Tech (nativetech.org/poetry) that lists works written by a range of Native poets.

Finally, Sherman Alexie, the popular author of novels, poetry, and screenplays such as *Smoke Signals* maintains a website at falls-apart.com. Alexie is remarkably prolific, and his site features a wide range of information about his books, recordings, and movies (all for sale on the site), as well as a useful "Academic" section that provides links to critical essays and other information about his work. However, there are no poems or other examples of Alexie's fictional work on the site; for these, visit the Hanksville.org site above.

OUT OF EMPIRE: BRITAIN AND ITS (FORMER) COLONIES

The extensive nature of British colonization in the 19th century and of the influence of U.S. commercial, military, and political power in the 20th means that, for better and for worse, English is the closest language to a global lingua franca. Three excellent and very comprehensive sites provide a wealth of information and poetry written in the British (post)colonial tradition and beyond. The Post Colonial Web (postcolonialweb.org) is organized by geographic region, and provides the best organized and most comprehensive survey of the literature, politics, geography, and history of every (former) British colony (except for the United States) of any online site today. The site is extremely easy to navigate, and the range and depth of links to information and other sites is excellent.

A close second to the Post Colonial Web, at least as far as its resources for the study of poetry, is ThePoetryHouse.org. This site is maintained by St. Andrews University in Scotland, and it, too, is organized by postcolonial region (including the United States), as a set of "rooms," each with its own editor. The first page of each room provides an overview of the poetry in that region, followed by a list of external links to various websites on the literature and poetry of that region. For example, the Canada room lists six links to resources on Canadian poetry, including a link at the University of Toronto and a Leonard Cohen "fansite."

A third, very interesting site is the Poetry Archive (www.poetryarchive.org). This is a British site specializing in recordings of poets reading their own work. Although the range of recordings is primarily British, it is not exclusively so, and features recordings of contemporary and past poets from Ireland, the United States, Canada, and all across the English-speaking world.

VOICES OF THE MIDDLE EAST
AND CENTRAL AND SOUTH ASIA

Four websites together provide substantial coverage of the poetry and poetic traditions of the region that stretches from Morocco in the far west across North Africa, north through Turkey, south through the Sudan, and eastward across the Levant, the Arabian peninsula, Iran, Central Asia, and the Indian subcontinent. Ohio University maintains perhaps the most comprehensive list of links featuring the poetry of Islam and the Middle East (ou.edu/mideast; click on "Categories"). As of this writing, 37 sites are featured. The sites are listed simply, with links and a one-sentence description. Some links are dead, but most work. A special focus of the site is the work of Rumi, a medieval Sufi poet. The site also contains many links to the poets and poetry of Turkey and Iran, as well as links to individual poets, such as Palestinian-American poet Naomi Shihab Nye.

A second site that focuses on the poetry of the Middle East can be found on the NewsHour page of the Public Broadcasting Service (pbs.org/newshour; search for "Middle East Poetry"). As part of its ongoing Poetry Series, the NewsHour recently featured a series of stories about Middle Eastern poetry, with particular emphasis on contemporary poets of Egypt, Lebanon, Palestine, and Israel. The resources on this site include videos of the stories that aired and of poets reading their own work in their native languages and in English translation.

I also recommend two other sites that feature the poetry of India. Kavitayan (geocities.com/kavitayan) offers an encyclopedic listing of the poets of India along with examples of the poetry of each. In addition, beyond the "first folio" (i.e., page of the site) there are samples of poetry in Urdu (in English translation) from Pakistan and essays on the poetry of the entire Indian subcontinent. This is a remarkable resource for teachers and students of all levels and interests. A second site is the page devoted to the work of Indian/Bengali poet and Nobel laureate Rabindranath Tagore (poemhunter.com; search poet's name). Tagore was a major literary figure in the first half of the 20th century (he won the Nobel Prize for Literature in 1913), but today is largely unknown within the context of the secondary English curriculum. He was a prolific writer whose work is surely as worthy of study today as that of his contemporaries, including Rudyard Kipling.

EAST ASIA

The poetry of East Asia, and particularly of China, Japan, Korea, and Vietnam, is well-represented on the Internet. The University of Virginia maintains two excellent sites that feature the classic poetry of China and Japan. The Chinese site (etext.virginia.edu/chinese) focuses on 300 poems from the Tang Dynasty, which is considered China's greatest literary period. The poems are presented in Chinese script with an English translation alongside it, with no commentary. A second site devoted to Chinese poetry is provided by China the Beautiful at chinapage.com/poetry. Again, these poems are presented singly, with no commentary. For information about particular Chinese poets and the Chinese poetic tradition, the Open Directory Project (dmoz.org; click on Arts, Literature, Poetry, Chinese) may provide the best introduction.

Several sites are fine sources of Japanese poetry. Again, the University of Virginia site (etext.virginia.edu/japanese) provides 100 classic tanka poems written by 100 Japanese poets, with a brief introduction about the form and its history. A second site with several poems is at classical-japanese.net/poetry. This unusual site features background information on Japanese poetry combined with lessons in simple animation techniques that are different from those described in Chapter 5. Finally, the National Endowment for the Humanities offers a site with information on how to teach the tanka form (edsitement.neh.gov; search for "tanka"); but you'll need to excuse the pun in its title.

Many other East Asian countries are not as well represented in English on the Internet. One site features the poetry of Wong Phui Nam, a Malaysian poet (viweb.freehosting.net/WongPN.htm). There are online scholarly articles written about Thai poetry, but I can find no sites with examples of poems. However, there are two interesting sites on the poetry of Vietnam and Korea. Le World at thehuuvandan.org provides multiple links on the poetry of Vietnam, particularly of three noted Vietnamese poets from the French colonial and postcolonial period: Jacques Nguyen Hieu Liem, Vo Thu Tinh, and Ly Lang Nhan. Another site, which contains the translations of Brother Anthony of Taize, provides many translations of Korean poetry into English and French at Hompi.sogang.ac.kr/anthony.

GLOBAL VOICES IN A HIGH-STAKES WORLD

Despite a good deal of rhetoric today on the part of politicians and policy makers about the need for U.S. schools to prepare students to be competitive in a global economy, efforts to internationalize school curriculum nationwide remain spotty and local at best. In my search of learning standards across multiple states, including New York, California, Illinois, Texas, Ohio, and Kentucky, I found almost no direct mention of comparative or international literature or even the literature of domestic multicultural groups in any state's reading or English language arts standards. Educators looking for standards that would directly support inclusion of poetry from the Middle East, Africa, Asia, Latin America, or even of African-American or Latina/o poets in their school curriculum are therefore likely to be frustrated and discouraged.

However, a broader reading of many states' curriculum documents would find that they do include standards mentioning the need for students to appreciate the linguistic and literary traditions of other nations and cultures. For example, Illinois Standard 2.A.5c calls for students to "Analyze the development of form (e.g., short stories, essays, speeches, poetry, plays, novels) and purpose in American literature and literature of other countries," and Standard 2.B.4b states that students should learn to "analyze form, content, purpose, and major themes of American literature and literature of other countries in their historical perspectives." The Kentucky middle-school standards for reading include a statement in the heading "Forming a Foundation for Reading" that mandates "reading at the word, sentence and connected text levels across content areas *that include multicultural texts* [emphasis added]." As a last example, the content standards for California do not specifically mention culture or national origin in those standards pertaining to teaching literature; however, in their introduction a list of "Recommended Literature, Kindergarten Through Grade Twelve" is mentioned. If you search this title on the California Department of Education website you will find a searchable list of authors and titles that includes not only African- and Asian-American and Latina/o literature but also appropriate titles and authors from Australia, Africa, Latin America, Europe, Russia, many countries in Central and East Asia, and every other inhabited part of the world. In other words, while support for reading multicultural and global literature is not

directly mentioned in most states' standards, neither is it prohib-
ited. Further, in many cases, an interpretive or deeper reading not
only of the standards but of the rationales for the standards suggests that many if not most state curriculum documents can be read
as supporting and even encouraging the use of literature that is
representative of cultures within that state, the nation, and around
the world.

KEEP IN MIND

- An even better source of poetry and information
  than the online sites discussed in this chapter may
  be immigrant or first-generation students and their
  parents. The surge in immigrants to the United States
  and Canada in the last 20 years from Asia, Latin
  America, Eastern Europe, and the Middle East means
  that today many schools and classrooms may have
  students from a wide variety of countries and cultures.
  Inviting the language and literature of all the students
  into your classroom, not only those from Britain or
  Northern Europe, is terribly important today. Imagine
  how much more welcome and at home a recently
  immigrated student or parent might feel if she or he
  were invited to come to your class one day to present
  a favorite poem or talk about the literary forms and
  traditions of her or his home country.
- Many of the websites discussed in this chapter offer
  poems both in their native language and script and in
  English translation. Taking advantage of this feature
  for work with English language learners, perhaps by
  asking them to translate or discuss the translation of a
  poem in their native language, is an excellent way to
  help them maintain their native language and develop
  proficiency in English literacy.
- The poetry of diverse cultural groups makes an
  excellent bridge to interdisciplinary study, particularly
  with geography and history. Poems can capture and
  represent the cultural and historical perspectives of the
  lives of Chinese immigrants during the California Gold

Rush, Japanese interns during World War II, Chicanos
along the border areas of the United States, or Africans
in the postcolonial period of the 1960s or 1970s with
greater intensity and expression than any textbook
discussion or essay might.

- Poetry from multicultural and international sources
  lends itself to many of the approaches described in
  this book, including Choral Reading (Chapter 1);
  the extension activities of Chapter 3, which focus
  on learning new poetic forms of expression; and the
  multimodal activities of Chapter 5. For example,
  following the model of the Favorite Poem Project,
  preservice teachers in my literacy methods courses
  have created "International Favorite Poem" videos, in
  which they ask a foreign-born student at the University
  of Illinois to recite a poem first in their native language,
  then in translation, and talk a bit about that poem's
  significance in their life and the life of their home
  culture.

Afterword

More than 30 years ago the first lesson I ever taught in a secondary classroom, returning as a 1st-year preservice teacher to his alma mater for his first field placement, was a poem: "To a Waterfowl," by William Cullen Bryant. I can't remember why I chose that poem; I didn't like it much myself, and it wasn't that my cooperating teacher had suggested it or had limited my choice of material in any way. I think I must have had some rationale, though, perhaps because it was relatively short, its meter and rhyme scheme were regular, and I figured I could say something about it that would sound like I knew what I was talking about.

I remember that teaching experience perfectly: I passed out copies, read the poem to the class, and tried quickly to identify its structure before launching into a series of "discussion questions" intended to lead the students to identify and ponder the metaphor of a waterfowl that surely unlocked the poem's "greatness." The lesson completely bombed. After a few minutes of droning I thought to look out at the class and noticed that most students had politely fallen asleep. I found myself floundering and beginning to stammer, unable to connect either to my audience or to my own train of thought. After a few minutes more I turned the class back over to my coop and fled the room, mortified with my own failure but also determined to figure out what I had done wrong and resolved never to let this happen to me or a class I was teaching again.

Over the years I periodically returned to teaching poetry and tried almost anything to get my students (and me) interested in its study. I tried poetry "units" and to get students to collect and write poems for personal anthologies; the students were cooperative in these activities but never fully engaged. I tried reciting poems myself and playing recordings of famous poets reading their own work, with little response. I even once taped copies of Shel Silverstein poems over the urinals in the boys' bathroom and on the stall doors of the girls', and got a huge laugh from everyone but very little close reading in return. It wasn't until I got over my own cultural hang-ups about poetry as "art" with "rules" that had to be memorized and submitted to and began to see poems as pieces of intense human expression that sprang from everyday life and which were the property of their readers and writers, rather than of teachers or critics, that productive ideas and teaching began to flow.

The approaches to teaching poetry I've described in this book are taken from this later period of my secondary teaching career and from my work as a teacher educator. When I began to assemble them for this book I was excited that they all seemed so different from one another and that I could actually order them so that they might progress in complexity and content from "basic" aspects of poetry education, like gaining an awareness of the relationship between rhyme and meaning to learning how to write and perform increasingly complicated forms to technology-mediated interpretations of poems that required sophisticated modes of analysis. Now at the end of the writing I am beginning to see what each approach has in common with the others—an analysis that also leads me to consider exactly what points a reader of this book who might be interested in experimenting for her- or himself with variations of these approaches or developing completely new approaches might want to consider. With this as my goal, I would like to conclude with five main points that any teachers interested in not just teaching but in getting themselves and their students excited to learn about poetry and poetic expression might want to keep in mind.

ONE: KEEP THE TEACHING PLAYFUL

Poetry is all about the *play* of language—about taking risks, trying new moves, and experimenting with language, all without serious consequence when things don't quite work out and with grand celebration when things do. This does not mean at all that its pursuit, whether as a reader or a writer, should not be serious or taken seriously, but that the spirit that surrounds learning about poetry has to be a spirit of freedom, a spirit free of stricture and harsh judgment. All too many times in my career I fear that I snatched failure from the jaws of success with my students because I pushed too hard or too long or insisted that some poetic form be followed to the letter from the start when I should have backed off and waited for success before I intervened with a "rule." Games do have rules, yes—otherwise, they would soon become anarchic and no fun at all—but rules exist to be negotiated and learned as part of the play itself.

TWO: KEEP THE POETRY RELEVANT

Yes, of course, this is true; but what makes something relevant? In this book I have repeatedly tried to make the point that finding poems that reflect the cultures and life experiences of the students in your classroom is critical to success in teaching poetry. I want to emphasize this point in conclusion but I also want to elaborate my criteria for relevance a bit. Hip-hop is an almost surefire way to induce contemporary youth to write poetry, but as both Marc Lamont Hill and Maisha Fisher have noted, it can also introduce students to a wide array of poetic devices that will serve as a bridge to reading other forms of poetry and using language with increasing power and precision. Its educational function, in other words, is not only to provide students with a culturally relevant approach to self-expression but to expand the range of texts that students may find relevant and interesting, and to provide students with the skills and the means to participate in an increasing number of literary and academic discourses.

With this goal in mind, I would therefore urge teachers of poetry to be continually expanding the boundaries of the poetic forms and topics that they introduce to their students, and to search for ways to bridge what students already know with what may be unfamiliar but potentially very engaging for them. That challenge can be met in a number of ways—for instance, by posing questions and issues in terms that are universal, or by finding poems from other cultures and nations that deal with familiar local problems or issues—but it must be met. Otherwise the teaching will not become transformative; it will meet students where they are and that's as far as they will go.

THREE: KEEP A FOCUS ON
PERFORMANCE AND PUBLICATION

All of the approaches discussed in this book succeed because they do not require students simply to read or write and talk abstractly *about* poetry, but rather to do something active and concrete *with* poems—mark them for a choral reading, write and play with them on paper, sing them as the blues, write them for reading and performance, or remix them multimodally. These activities push students to use not only their minds but also their bodies and an expanding repertoire of cultural practices. And they move poetry from an individual to a highly social, deeply cultural activity that builds confidence and identities as literate, smart, public personalities. Performance and/or publication are absolutely critical, then, not only to teaching poetry but to reaping the educational and social benefits that being a poet and a critic of poetry brings.

FOUR: KEEP YOUR TEACHING
ANALYTICAL AND RIGOROUS

Throughout this book I have stressed that even as it is critical to maintain a playful, culturally relevant, and performative approach to teaching poetry, it also remains true that the most lasting and transformative learning comes from the analysis—the debriefing and reflexive discussion—that comes after the performance or publication of a poem, when students are pressed to explore their own reasoning processes and use new terms and concepts. I am not suggesting at all that the ultimate goal of these approaches is to develop the reading practices of New Criticism. But I am suggesting that to grow and develop as poets students must also develop a poet's technical mastery of language and poetic form, which includes a knowledge of terms and a wide repertoire of poems. Moreover, without extended analysis and debriefing of students' experiences, many if not most of the standards that justify the teaching of poetry bureaucratically would not be met. In other words, engaging students in the fun of writing and performing is only half the task of teaching; the other half is to channel that engagement in the service of formal language study in ways that build students' confidence and knowledge base without turning the learning process into hard labor.

FIVE: MAKE TECHNOLOGY YOUR FRIEND

We live in a multimodal world, in which the most influential and pervasive texts, now and forevermore, are likely to be those that combine print with still images, video, and sound in exciting ways. New genres are under development now that will blend reading and writing with listening and speaking almost seamlessly. Print and print literacy are not likely to disappear in this process, but focusing exclusively on learning to read and write print without also attending to the visual and auditory aspects of a text will begin to seem at first quaintly anachronistic and then hopelessly dated and irrelevant as the century progresses.

In short, depending on which side of the technological revolution a teacher stands it is either the most exciting time in centuries to teach the English language arts or it is the end of the profession. Teaching poetry should not provide a refuge from the coming changes in literate expression; it should be an opportunity to expand instructional repertoires and to break new ground through a wide range of computer-based resources. That is why the vast majority of resources listed in this book are available online rather than printed works listed in the References section at the end of the book, and why the book's accompanying website is so vital to making full use of this printed text. In closing, then, I want to remind readers of the mantra of Chapter 5: You can't break software, and everything can be fixed. That is the beauty of the virtual world of technology, and my final invitation to teachers: Take the time to experiment online and at your computer; be humble enough to admit you're a learner yourself in this new world, and ask your students for help when you screw up.

References

Ackerman, M. B. (1968). Why I don't teach poetry. *English Journal, 57,* 999–1001.

Chandler, F. W. (1915). A creative approach to the study of literature. *English Journal, 4,* 281–291.

Cobbs, L. (2005). Learning to listen, listening to learn: Teaching poetry as a sensory medium. *English Journal, 94,* 28–32.

Dreher, P. (2000). Electronic poetry: Student-constructed hypermedia. *English Journal, 90,* 68–73.

Eaton, H. (1913). Reading poetry aloud. *English Journal, 2,* 151–157.

Escher, E. (2006). *The rapper's handbook: A guide to freestyling, writing rhymes, and battling.* New York: Flocabulary Press.

Fisher, M. T. (2007). *Writing in rhythm: Spoken word poetry in urban classrooms.* New York: Teachers College Press.

Fleischman, P., & Beddows, E. (2004). *Joyful noise: Poems for two voices.* New York: HarperCollins.

Fleischman, P., & Giacobbe, B. (2008). *Big talk: Poems for four voices.* Somerville, MA: Candlewick Press.

Fleischman, P., & Nutt, K. (1989). *I am phoenix: Poems for two voices.* New York: HarperCollins.

Giovanni, N. (1972). *My house.* New York: Morrow.

Giovanni, N. (Ed.). (2008). *Hip-hop speaks to children: A celebration of poetry with a beat.* Naperville, IL: Sourcebooks Jabberwocky.

Glicksberg, C. (1940). Creative experiences and experiments in an English classroom. *English Journal, 29,* 533–542.

Gutteridge, D. (1972). The affective fallacy and the student's response to poetry. *English Journal, 61,* 210–221.

Hill, M. L. (2009). *Beats, rhymes, and classroom life: Hip-hop pedagogy and the politics of identity.* New York: Teachers College Press.

Jonassen, D. H., Peck, K. L., & Wilson, B. G. (1999). *Learning with technology: A constructivist perspective.* Upper Saddle River, NJ: Prentice Hall.

Loar, G. (1932). A verse-speaking choir in high school. *English Journal, 21,* 710–715.

McVee, M. B., Bailey, N. M., & Shanahan, L. E. (2008). Using digital media to interpret poetry: Spiderman meets Walt Whitman. *Research in the Teaching of English, 43,* 112–143.

Nelson, C. (Ed.). (2000). *Anthology of American poetry.* New York: Oxford University Press.

Paredes, A. (1958). *"With his pistol in his hand": A border ballad and its hero.* Austin: The University of Texas Press.

Paul, H. G. (1912). The teaching of lyric poetry. *English Journal, 1,* 466–475.

Renz, B. (1936). Teaching poetry through oral interpretation. *English Journal, 25,* 561–566.

Saïd, E. (1993). *Culture and imperialism.* New York: Vintage.

Index

About the Author

Mark Dressman is an associate professor in the Department of Curriculum and Instruction at the University of Illinois at Urbana-Champaign, where he teaches courses in secondary English methods and qualitative research. Dressman began his career teaching English in the Peace Corps in Morocco. He has also taught on the Navajo Indian Reservation and in the Cincinnati Public Schools. He is currently also an editor of *Research in the Teaching of English.*